dancing
dragonfly
QUILTS

12 CAPTIVATING PROJECTS ◆ DESIGN & PIECING OPTIONS ◆ 6 BLOCK VARIATIONS

SUE BEEVERS

C&T PUBLISHING

D0752266

Text copyright © 2009 by Sue Beevers

Artwork copyright © 2009 by C&T Publishing, Inc.

Publisher: Amy Marson

Creative Director: Gailen Runge

Editors: Jake Finch and Stacy Chamness

Technical Editors: Helen Frost and Amanda Siegfried

Copyeditor/Proofreader: Wordfirm Inc.

Cover/Book Designer: Christina D. Jarumay

Production Coordinators: Casey Dukes and Kirstie Pettersen

Illustrator: Gregg Valley

Photography by Christina Carty-Francis and Diane Pedersen
of C&T Publishing, Inc., unless otherwise noted.

Published by C&T Publishing, Inc., P.O. Box 1456, Lafayette,
CA 94549

All rights reserved. No part of this work covered by the
copyright hereon may be used in any form or reproduced
by any means—graphic, electronic, or mechanical, including
photocopying, recording, taping, or information storage
and retrieval systems—without written permission from the
publisher. The copyrights on individual artworks are retained
by the artists as noted in *Dancing Dragonfly Quilts*. These
designs may be used to make items only for personal use or
donation to nonprofit groups for sale. Each piece of finished
merchandise for sale must carry a conspicuous label with
the following information: Designs copyright © 2009 by Sue
Beevers from the book *Dancing Dragonfly Quilts* from C&T
Publishing, Inc.

Attention Copy Shops: Please note the following exception—
publisher and author give permission to photocopy pages
11–16, 32, 33, 35 for personal use only.

Attention Teachers: C&T Publishing, Inc., encourages you
to use this book as a text for teaching. Contact us at
800-284-1114 for more information about the C&T Teachers'
Program.

We take great care to ensure that the information included
in our products is accurate and presented in good faith, but
no warranty is provided nor are results guaranteed. Having
no control over the choices of materials or procedures used,
neither the author nor C&T Publishing, Inc., shall have any
liability to any person or entity with respect to any loss or
damage caused directly or indirectly by the information
contained in this book. For your convenience, we post an
up-to-date listing of corrections on our website (www.ctpub.
com). If a correction is not already noted, please contact our
customer service department at ctinfo@ctpub.com or at P.O.
Box 1456, Lafayette, CA 94549.

Trademark (™) and registered trademark (®) names are used
throughout this book. Rather than use the symbols with
every occurrence of a trademark or registered trademark
name, we are using the names only in the editorial fashion
and to the benefit of the owner, with no intention of
infringement.

Library of Congress Cataloging-in-Publication Data

Beevers, Sue

 Dancing dragonfly quilts : 12 captivating projects—design &
piecing options—6 block variations / Sue Beevers.

  p. cm.

 Summary: "All the instruction you need to create dazzling
new quilts from the traditional Dragonfly block is here in this
comprehensive workbook. Try any of the 12 complete quilt
projects, or use Sue's design techniques to make your own
original Dragonfly designs"—Provided by publisher.

 ISBN 978-1-57120-561-2 (paper trade : alk. paper)

 1. Patchwork—Patterns. 2. Quilting—Patterns. 3.
Dragonflies in art. I. Title.

 TT835.B3768 2009

 746.46'041--dc22

                              2008036392

Printed in China

10 9 8 7 6 5 4 3 2

ACKNOWLEDGMENTS

*Writing a book is never done alone; many people and businesses have
helped me.*

*First of all, I would like to thank Jan Grigsby. Her advice, encouragement,
and suggestions have been invaluable. I also thank my editors Stacy
Chamness and Jake Finch, technical editors Helen Frost and Amanda
Siegfried, and illustrator Gregg Valley. Without them, this book would
not be.*

*I would also like to thank RJR Fabrics. They are wonderful to work with.
Many of the beautiful fabrics in the quilts come from them, including
the amazing silk and velveteen fabrics. In particular, I would like to
thank Demetria Hayward for all of her help and encouragement.*

*Thank you to the folks at Janome. It is a real treat to use a sewing
machine that is so user-friendly. I especially love the fact that I don't
have to wrestle with large quilts in order to quilt them.*

*I would like to thank Vicki Paullus and the folks at Mountain Mist for
providing the quilt batting in the quilts. It is truly a joy to work with
beautiful batting that easily stays put when sandwiching a quilt and is
user-friendly when quilting. I've fallen in love with their silk/cotton blend
batting, and their Eco-Friendly batting is delightful.*

*I would like to thank Patti Lee at Sulky for the incredibly beautiful
variegated threads that were used for quilting. They add so much to
the quilts and are a joy to work with.*

*Thank you to Kathryn Stenstrom, Gail Strout, Anne Kinnel, Paula
Schultz, Margaret Willemsen, and Sue Ellen Romanowski for their
wonderful quilts. Aren't they beautiful?*

*Thank you to my son, Brien, my resident computer geek. My computer
fried a month and a half before the book's deadline. It is thanks to him
that this event wasn't a disaster of major proportions!*

*Thank you to my daughter, Anne, for all of her suggestions, encourage-
ment, and perspective about life.*

*And most of all, thank you to my husband, David. It is truly a gift to
have someone say, "You can do anything that you put your mind to,"
and then do everything possible to ensure that you have the time to
do it. Amazing!*

DEDICATION

For Mary Ann Stiefvater.
Sisters always.

CONTEN

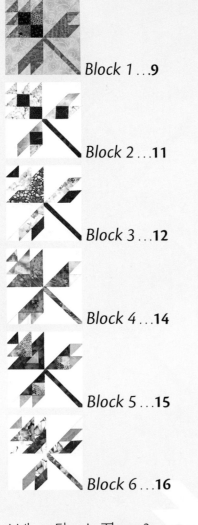

T S

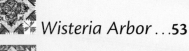

QUILT DESIGNS

INTRODUCTION

I am not a traditional quilter—at least I don't think of myself as such.

It's not that I don't love traditional quilts, because I do. It's just that whenever I start a quilt, it takes on a life of its own and moves in a direction that I never expected.

I think this mostly happens because I don't cut all of my fabric pieces out before sewing. This allows me to have more flexibility when making fabric and color decisions. It also allows me to live with the quilt and to listen to what it is telling me. And often it is telling me to change direction midstream.

So this book is about what happens when a traditional pattern transforms and becomes part of a not-so-traditional quilt.

the blocks

The Original Dragonfly Pattern

In 2007, my friend Gail Strout organized a quilt exhibit for the local historical society. One quilt, circa 1860–1880, stuck in my mind because the pattern had so much potential for modification. It was composed of four blocks: a bear-paw-ish head, a wing block that mirrored itself, and a tail block. I copied the block and immediately started thinking, "What if?"

My original Dragonfly quilt block

The original quilt block consisted of two colors: one used for the motif and off-white for the background. The motif fabrics, made up of mostly brown prints, varied from block to block, but individual blocks contained only one patterned fabric.

The pieced block in the quilt always faced the same direction and alternated with plain background squares of the same size. There was no attempt to sort the blocks by value, and sometimes blocks containing the same fabric were placed side by side. It was a very simple, yet quite effective design, and one I couldn't resist. I went home and made my own traditional quilt.

My version of the original quilt made with Dragonfly blocks

This is such an intriguing block. Although it is fairly simple, the opportunities for color variations are numerous. And best of all, the block reads well on any background: light, medium, or dark.

Dragonfly block on medium-green background by Anne Kinnel

The background fabrics need not be the same. Actually, as long as there is contrast between the Dragonfly fabrics and the background fabrics, the finished block will be successful.

Dragonfly block with light background and medium body fabrics by Anne Kinnel

Another feature of this block that I find interesting is that the head square and wing triangles are plain. To me, they are a blank palette for stitched designs or appliqué motifs.

Simple machine-stitched designs add interest to the quilt block.

Finally, and the best part as far as I'm concerned, the block is symmetrical on only one axis and has a diagonal orientation. This allows for a wealth of visual variations when the blocks are set in a quilt. All in all, this is a very interesting quilt block.

This book takes this wonderful Dragonfly block and shows you how you can manipulate and change what it was originally into something even better. It's really a workshop between pages to enable you to experiment with this block and its placement in your quilts. Most of the principles and exercises here can be used to redesign many other traditional blocks. You are only limited by your imagination!

Modifying the Dragonfly Block

One of the more interesting features of this block is its simplicity. This means that additional squares, triangles, and appliqué motifs can be added to the block without destroying the original motif.

The original Dragonfly block has four different components: the head, left wing, right wing, and tail.

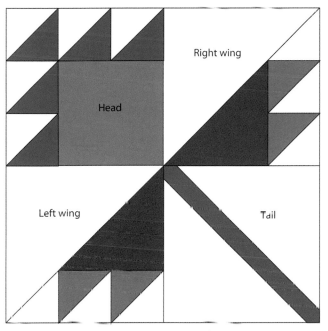

Illustration of the original block

The wings are always mirror images of each other. The tail is a simple diagonal line. Together these components create a symmetrical block with a diagonal orientation. This orientation creates a sense of movement within the block: it points in a diagonal direction. In order to preserve the integrity of the motif, it is important to maintain this diagonal movement when modifying the block.

BLOCK 1

When the head square of the original pattern is divided into four smaller squares, myriad design possibilities open up.

Block 1 with four smaller head squares by Anne Kinnel

The squares can be subdivided into even smaller squares for a checkerboard effect.

Block 1 with 16 smaller head squares by Sue Ellen Romanowski

The squares can also be subdivided into triangles, which can then be turned to create a Pinwheel motif.

Block 1 with Pinwheel block for head by Sue Ellen Romanowski

A series of triangles can form a Flying Geese motif.

Block 1 with Flying Geese head block by Sue Ellen Romanowski

Because there are four smaller blocks in the head section, radiating patterns can easily be formed. If you look at *Sparkling Spring Afternoon* (page 50), you will see an example of a rotated image forming a radiating pattern.

Block 1 with rotated image in head block

The process is simple:

1. Isolate a motif in the fabric. The motif does not have to be symmetrical.

Pick a fabric to draw a motif from.

Isolate a motif in the fabric.

2. Cut 4 identical motifs. The easiest way is to cut a motif, then place it on top of the same motif in the fabric, carefully aligning the design so it appears as if it's the same piece of fabric. Don't forget to allow ¼" on all sides for the seam allowance. If the outer edges of the cut motif match those of the underlying fabric, it is safe to cut the next square.

3. Place the 4 squares on a table, and orient the motifs so that they point either inward or outward.

Four identical sections are selected from the motif fabric.

4. Sew the squares together, and proceed with constructing the block.

Cutting the squares from a symmetrical motif will create a kaleidoscope-like effect. Or try fussy cutting any motif so it is centered within the square. This will create a lovely visual effect for your block.

Block 1 with fussy-cut motifs by Anne Kinnel

These are just a few suggestions, and I'm sure that you have some more ideas at this point, so here are some blank blocks for you to play with. Get out your crayons or colored pencils and have some fun!

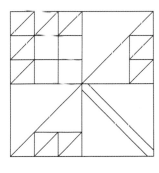
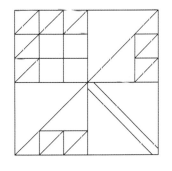
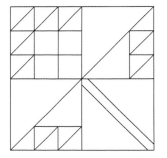
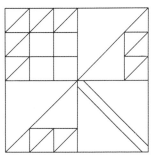

Block 1 blanks

BLOCK 2

The simple addition of two diagonal squares in the head section creates the illusion of a continuous diagonal line from the head through the tail.

Block 2 with two diagonal squares

This effect is emphasized when the tail and head square fabrics are the same.

Block 2 with the same fabric for head squares, tail, and wing squares by Sue Ellen Romanowski

Additionally, when the squares are color gradated, a strong sense of movement occurs.

Block 2 with color gradations by Kathryn Stenstrom

This variation of the quilt block also adds squares to the wings. The quadrilateral that is formed creates a sense of an upper and lower wing, an effect that can be enhanced by color placement. The color placement also affects the way in which the upper and lower wings orient to each other.

Block 2 with squares on the wings by Anne Kinnel

Don't forget that these smaller squares can also become a blank palette for appliqué or machine-stitched designs.

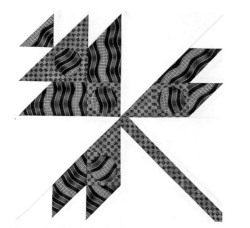

Block 2 with appliquéd circles in the squares by Kathryn Stenstrom

It's time again to get out your crayons and colored pencils and have some fun! Here are some blank blocks for you to play with.

Block 2 blanks

Don't forget that the color placement and the number of colors used in the motif can make the motif appear to be quite geometric. Remember that in the long run, simpler is often the better choice!

BLOCK 3

This variation of the original Dragonfly block creates the illusion of overlapping triangles in the head section, while adding quadrilaterals to the wings. The result is a block that is deceptively simple.

Block 3 with overlapping triangles in the head section

Even when only one color is used, it can be quite effective.

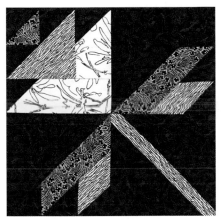

Block 3 in black-and-white fabrics by Anne Kinnel

And yet, there are many opportunities for color variations. Add a second color for a fair amount of variation.

Block 3 with color variations by Gail Strout

As you can imagine, more colors provide even more opportunities to alter the look of the block. Don't forget that contrasting colors can be used to highlight a specific portion of the block.

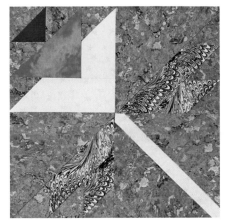

Block 3 variation with light fabric producing a chevron by Sue Ellen Romanowski

Try it out for yourself. You'll be surprised at how many color variations you can generate.

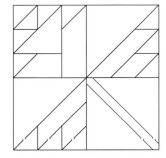
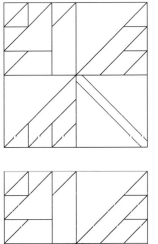
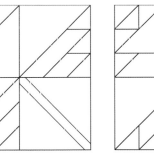
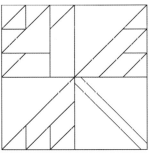

Block 3 blanks

BLOCK 4

The previous block variation created the illusion of the head made up of overlapping triangles. This block combines those triangles with the squares used in Block 2. Also, the trapezoids from the head block are echoed in the wings. This makes the wings appear wider than those in Block 3. In reality, both are exactly the same size.

Block 4 is made up of squares and triangles in the head section.

Color is always important in defining individual block pieces. But in this particular block, the pieces themselves create an almost southwestern feel. Using colors that are usually associated with that part of the country accentuates the illusion.

Block 4 variation made with colors of the Southwest by Gail Strout

This block appears to be complex because of the orientation of the pieces. In such a situation, I find that allowing the fabric to create texture and complexity is more successful than subdividing some motifs into smaller motifs.

Block 4 by Kathryn Stenstrom appears more complex because of the fabric's texture.

But it's up to you. Here is another set of blanks for you to experiment with.

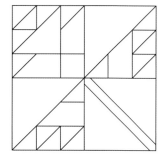
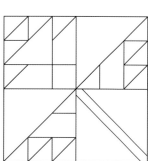
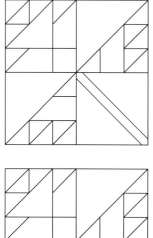
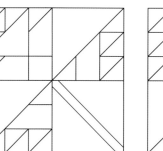

Block 4 blanks

BLOCK 5

This variation of the Dragonfly block has "nesting triangles" in the head section, which create the illusion of a small triangle floating within the larger triangle. As you can well imagine, this creates a lot of opportunities for color variations.

Block 5 is made with nesting triangles.

To construct the block more easily, you will need to divide the bottom triangle. This gives the option of dividing the large triangle with a wide band through the placement of color.

Block 5 has other variations on the nesting triangle created by color choice.

You'll note that the wings are composed entirely of triangles and squares. This appears to be a very complex block with a lot of opportunities for color variations.

Block 5 black variation by Gail Strout

Block 5 navy blue variation by Gail Strout

Here are some blanks for you to try out your own color ideas. Have fun!

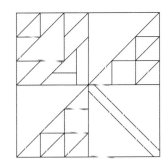
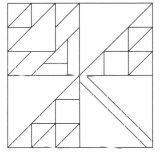
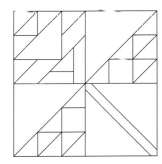
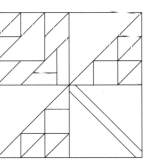

Block 5 blanks

BLOCK 6

This final variation of the Dragonfly block is created from triangles and trapezoids. Contrasting colors will emphasize the effect of a striped motif. It's an interesting block because it has diagonals in opposing directions: the diagonal created by the motif itself and the diagonals within the motif.

Block 6 made with triangles and trapezoids, which creates a striped effect

Color can be used to accentuate or minimize this effect.

Block 6 color variations by Gail Strout. Color variations can change the striped effect.

This is a great block if you want to add smaller geometric motifs to the wings and head. Obviously, the motifs' placement and color will accentuate or minimize the diagonals, but they can also create directional changes. It's a fun variation of the original block.

Block 6 by Anne Kinnel uses Flying Geese in wings and head in opposing directions

Here are a few blank blocks for you to experiment with.

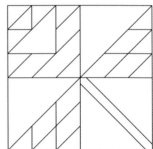
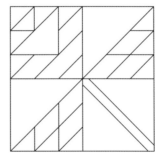
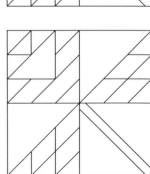
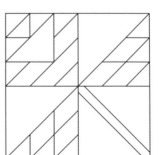

Block 6 blanks

What Else Is There?

As you've been experimenting with the various Dragonfly blocks, you've probably realized that the potential for variation is enormous. Alter the general appearance of the block by adding squares, triangles, and trapezoids.

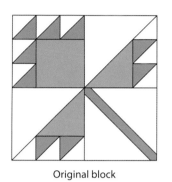

Original block

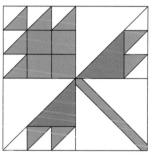

Block 1

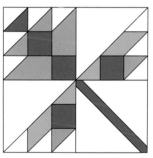

Block 2

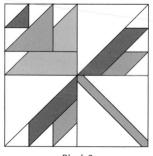

Block 3

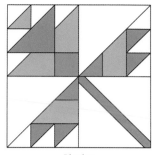

Block 4

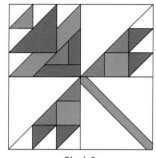

Block 5

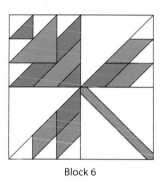

Block 6

Overview of Dragonfly blocks

You've also discovered that color variations can emphasize or hide block motifs: small geometric designs can be added to the block's motifs, and large plain spaces can be embroidered or appliquéd. There's a lot to think about and a lot of sewing fun ahead for you!

piecing the blocks

What Size Do I Make the Block?

It's a simple question, and a good one. Three factors control the block's size:

1. The finished size of the quilt

2. The number of blocks in the quilt

3. The method of block construction

You will find more information about determining the finished size of your quilt, including sashing, border bands, and bindings, in Chapter 4. You will find information about deciding on the block layout in Chapter 3.

All of the Dragonfly blocks are basically four-patch blocks. Each of those patches can be subdivided into nine equal smaller squares. Subdivide one smaller square into sixteen squares to find the sizes for the tail pieces. This is a very important proportion to maintain, as a wider tail makes the block appear heavy. A narrower tail is just too skinny to be visually appealing in relation to the other block pieces. Although the illustration shows the original block, all block variations and modifications are based on these subdivisions, and it is important to always maintain these proportions.

Basically, a block is six squares wide by six squares long. Therefore, a block can be any size that is a multiple of six.

For example, if each of the smallest squares is 1", the finished block will be 6". If the smallest square is ½", the finished block will be 3".

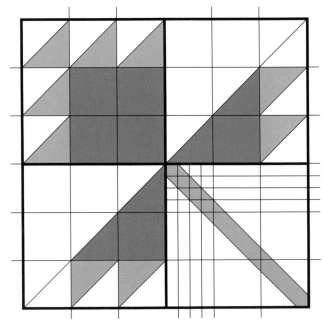

Dragonfly blocks are basically four-patch blocks.

Small Square Size	Finished Block Size
1"	6"
1¼"	7½"
1½"	9"
1¾"	10½"
2"	12"
2¼"	13½"
2½"	15"
2¾"	16½"
3"	18"
3¼"	19½"
3½"	21"
3¾"	22½"
4"	24"

Constructing the Blocks

The original Dragonfly block and all of its variations can be pieced three different ways:

■ Traditional piecing

■ Template piecing

■ Paper piecing

One way isn't necessarily better than another; everyone has preferences. Find the method that works best for you, and follow the piecing instructions. Join the pieced sections to make the block. The following piecing instructions work for traditional pieced, template-pieced, and paper-pieced blocks.

Always press carefully after each piece is sewn. Pressing after each step will make your piecing more precise.

ORIGINAL BLOCK

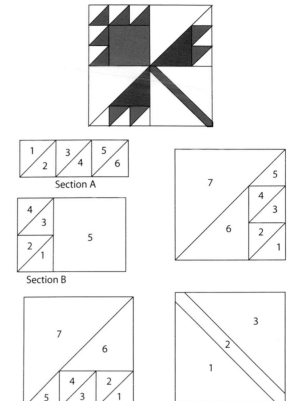

Original Dragonfly block piecing order

HEAD

1. Section A: Sew pieces 1 through 6 together in order. Press and set aside.

2. Section B: Sew pieces 1 through 4 together. Then sew Section B to piece 5.

3. Sew Sections A and B together.

WINGS

The right and left wings are mirror images of each other.

1. Sew pieces 1 through 5 together in order. Press.

2. Sew this unit to piece 6. Press.

3. Sew the entire unit to piece 7. Press.

TAIL

Sew pieces 1 through 3 together as shown in the diagram. Shape the ends of piece 2 to form right angles.

BLOCK 1

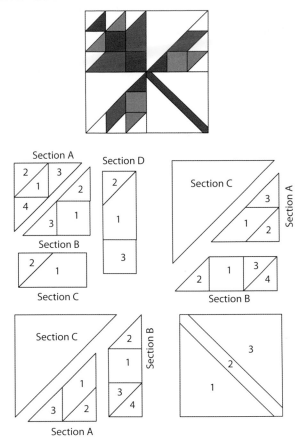

Dragonfly Block 1 piecing order

HEAD

1. Section A: Sew pieces 1 through 6 together in order. Press and set aside.

2. Section B: Sew pieces 1 through 4 together. Press and set aside.

3. Section C: Sew pieces 1 through 4 together. Even if you are paper piecing, this section is conventionally pieced. Press carefully, and sew to Section B. Press.

4. Sew Section A to Section B/C.

WINGS

The right and left wings are mirror images of each other.

1. Sew pieces 1 through 5 together in order. Press.

2. Sew these pieces to piece 6. Press.

3. Sew entire group to piece 7. Press.

TAIL

Sew pieces 1 through 3 together as shown in the diagram. Shape the ends of piece 2 to form right angles.

BLOCK 2

Dragonfly Block 2 piecing order

HEAD

1. Section A: Sew pieces 1 through 4 together in order. Press and set aside.

2. Section B: Sew pieces 1 through 3 together. Press and sew to Section A. You now have a small pieced square. Set aside.

3. Section C: Sew pieces 1 and 2 together. Press and then sew to the bottom of the small pieced square. Press and set aside.

4. Section D: Sew pieces 1 through 3 together. Press and then sew to the side of the previously pieced sections. Press.

WINGS

The right and left wings are mirror images of each other.

1. Section A: Sew pieces 1 through 3 together in order. Press and set aside.

2. Section B: Sew pieces 1 through 4 together. Press. Sew Sections A and B together.

3. Sew entire group to Section C. Press.

TAIL

Sew pieces 1 through 3 together as shown in the diagram. Shape the ends of piece 2 to form right angles.

BLOCK 3

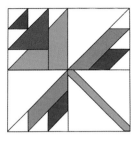

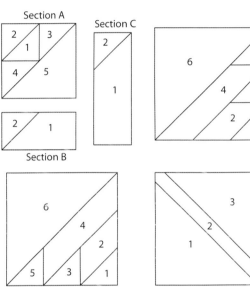

Dragonfly Block 3 piecing order

HEAD

1. Section A: Sew pieces 1 through 5 together in order. Press and set aside.

2. Section B: Sew pieces 1 and 2 together. Press and sew to Section A. Press and set aside.

3. Section C: Sew pieces 1 and 2 together. Press carefully. Then sew to the previously sewn sections. Press.

WINGS

The right and left wings are mirror images of each other.

Sew pieces 1 through 6 together in order. Press.

TAIL

Sew pieces 1 through 3 together as shown in the diagram. Shape the ends of piece 2 to form right angles.

BLOCK 4

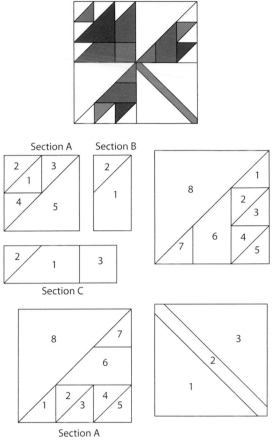

Dragonfly Block 4 piecing order

HEAD

1. Section A: Sew pieces 1 through 5 together in order. Press and set aside.

2. Section B: Sew pieces 1 and 2 together. Press and sew to Section A. Press and set aside.

3. Section C: Sew pieces 1 through 3 together. Press carefully. Then sew to the previously sewn sections. Press.

WINGS

The right and left wings are mirror images of each other.

Sew pieces 1 through 8 together in order. Press.

TAIL

Sew pieces 1 through 3 together as shown in the diagram. Shape the ends of piece 2 to form right angles.

BLOCK 5

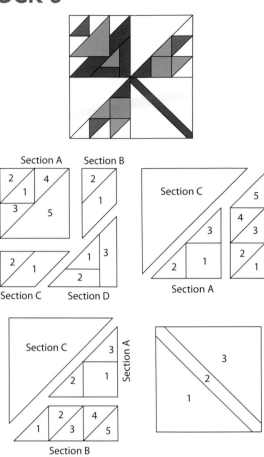

Dragonfly Block 5 piecing order

HEAD

1. Section A: Sew pieces 1 through 5 together in order. Press and set aside.

2. Section B: Sew pieces 1 and 2 together. Press and sew to Section A. Press and set aside.

3. Section C: Sew pieces 1 and 2 together. Press carefully. Then sew to the previously sewn sections. Press and set aside.

4. Section D: Sew pieces 1 through 3 together in order. Press and sew to the previously pieced sections.

WINGS

The left and right wings are mirror images of each other.

1. Section A: Sew pieces 1 through 3 together in order. Press and set aside.

2. Section B: Sew pieces 1 through 5 together in order. Press and sew to Section A. Press.

3. Section C: Sew this section to the previously pieced sections. Press.

TAIL

Sew the 3 pieces together as shown in the diagram. Shape the ends of piece 2 to form right angles.

BLOCK 6

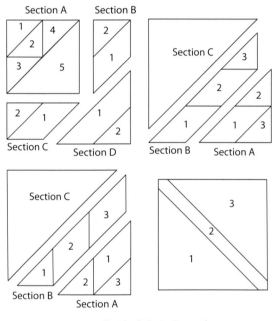

Dragonfly Block 6 piecing order

HEAD

1. Section A: Sew pieces 1 through 5 together in order. Press and set aside.

2. Section B: Sew pieces 1 and 2 together. Press and sew to Section A. Press and set aside.

3. Section C: Sew pieces 1 and 2 together. Press carefully. Then sew to the previously sewn sections. Press.

4. Section D: Sew pieces 1 and 2 together. Press carefully. Then sew to the previously pieced sections.

WINGS

The left and right wings are mirror images of each other.

1. Section A: Sew pieces 1 through 3 together in order. Press and set aside.

2. Section B: Sew pieces 1 through 3 together in order. Press and sew to Section A. Press.

3. Section C: Sew this section to the previously pieced sections.

TAIL

Sew the 3 pieces together as shown in the diagram. Shape the ends of piece 2 to form right angles.

Cutting Sizes

TRADITIONAL PIECING

Cutting sizes for the traditional pieced blocks are quite easy to figure out. Follow these steps to calculate your cutting needs:

1. Determine the finished size of the block.

2. Determine the size of the small square in each block.

3. If the edge has a right (90°) angle, add a ¼″ seam allowance on that side.

4. If the edge has a 45° angle, add a ⅝″ seam allowance on that side.

So practically speaking, if the piece has 90° angles all around, add ½″ for the seam allowance. If it has a 90° angle and a 45° angle, add a ⅞″ seam allowance. If it has two 45° angles, add 1¼″ for the seam allowance. Needless to say, you must sew the seams with an exact ¼″ seam, or your pieces will not fit together correctly.

tip

There is an exception to this rule. If the sizes of the pieces in the block are quite small—under 1½″ finished size—you will want to use a scant ¼″ seam allowance. This is because there is always some take-up at the seams, and small pieces by their very nature have less stretch and are therefore less forgiving of the seams.

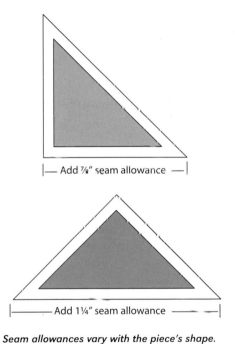

|–Add ½″ seam allowance–|

|— Add ⅞″ seam allowance —|

|——— Add 1¼″ seam allowance ———|

Seam allowances vary with the piece's shape.

HALF-SQUARE OR QUARTER-SQUARE TRIANGLES?

Whether to use half-square or quarter-square triangles is up to you. It depends on which way you want the straight of grain—the direction of the woven thread in the fabric—to fall. If you want it to be along one of the short sides, you will use a half-square triangle. If the straight of grain falls along the diagonal line of the triangle, you will use a quarter-square triangle. Dragonfly quilt blocks mostly use half-square triangles.

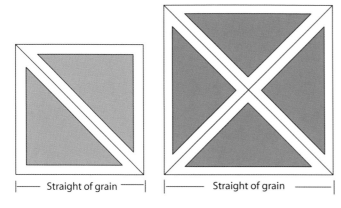

Half- and quarter-square triangle straight-of-grain placement

MEASURING TRAPEZOIDS

All of the trapezoids in these blocks have 90° and 45° angles. Add ½″ to the finished measurement of the side with two 90° angles. Add ⅞″ to the side with the 90° and 45° angles.

The trapezoids in the blocks always mirror each other. Cut half of the trapezoids for each block angling to the right and half angling to the left. Or simply cut them from two layers of fabric folded wrong sides together.

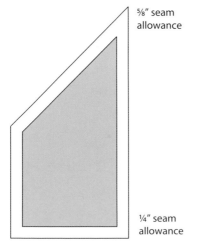

Trapezoid seam allowances

MEASURING QUADRILATERALS

Block 6 uses a quadrilateral piece. Each end has a 45° angle. Add ½″ to the finished measurement of the width and 1¼″ to the length.

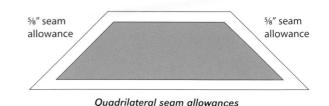

Quadrilateral seam allowances

PARALLELOGRAM CUTTING SIZES

Several blocks use parallelograms. Each end has a 45° angle. Add ½″ to the finished measurement of the width and 1¼″ to the length.

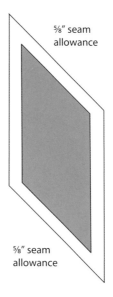

Parallelogram seam allowances

The parallelograms used in the blocks always mirror each other. Cut half of the parallelograms for each block angling to the right and half angling to the left. Or simply cut them from two layers of fabric folded wrong sides together.

TEMPLATE PIECING

The fabric amounts for a template-pieced block will be the same as its corresponding traditional-pieced block. But there is an advantage to template piecing: very little measuring is needed.

Simply follow these steps:

1. Plan the finished measurements for the block.

2. Draw the block in its finished size.

> ### tip
> This drawing must be exact, because this is what you will base your templates on. Graph paper works well. If you are drawing a large block, you may find it necessary to tape a couple of pieces of paper together. Draw the entire block at once. Drawing one piece at a time can create inaccuracies.

3. Trace the outline of the individual pieces on template plastic. Use a ruler and a permanent marker. Pencil and ballpoint pen will rub off. Don't forget to label each piece—for example, "Block 2: Upper left wing trapezoid." If there is any question about the straight-of-grain line, mark it on the template.

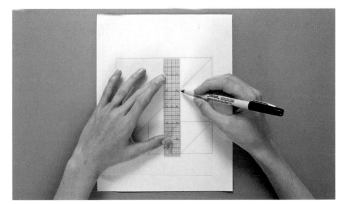

Trace piece outline onto template plastic using a ruler.

> ### tip
> If you have any question about the writing implement that you're using, scribble a bit on the template plastic and wait about five minutes. If it rubs off, use a different pen. I use a pencil.

4. Add ¼" seam allowance around the outside edge of each individual piece using a ruler.

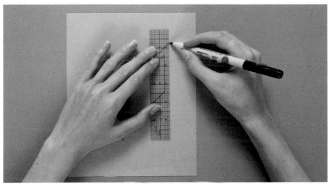

Add seam allowance using a ruler.

5. Cut out the template using a ruler and a rotary cutter. Make sure your blade is very sharp.

6. Cutting fabric pieces using a template is easy. Orient the template on the straight of grain of the fabric. Place a ruler over the template, matching the ¼" line of the ruler with the outline of the piece, and cut with a rotary cutter.

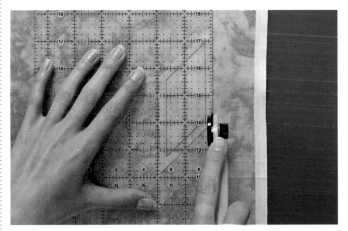

Using a template

> ### tip
> Remember to draw the initial block and the traced pieces as accurately as possible on the template! If the measurements are off, the quilt block will be incorrect.

Quick & Easy Paper Piecing

The advantages of paper piecing are obvious:

1. No careful measuring is needed. Because you are working with a pre-printed pattern, the measuring has already been done.

2. Resizing the pattern is simple. Scan the pattern into the computer, or take it to your local copy store.

3. The block can be any size. You aren't tied to a block size that can easily be measured.

4. Piecing small pieces is always accurate. All you have to do is follow the stitching line.

Why wouldn't everyone want to paper piece? Well, the process might have seemed difficult and confusing. But there is a simple way to paper piece. If you've been turned off by paper piecing in the past, I urge you to try it my way.

PAPER PIECING STEPS

1. Determine block size from the finished quilt size. Draw out the block in the appropriate size. Don't forget that the Dragonfly block has four sections: head, left wing, right wing, and tail. Each section is pieced separately.

2. Determine what color and type of fabric each piece will be. Write it on the pattern. For example, in each small head triangle, write "light green floral." Number each piece to show the piecing order.

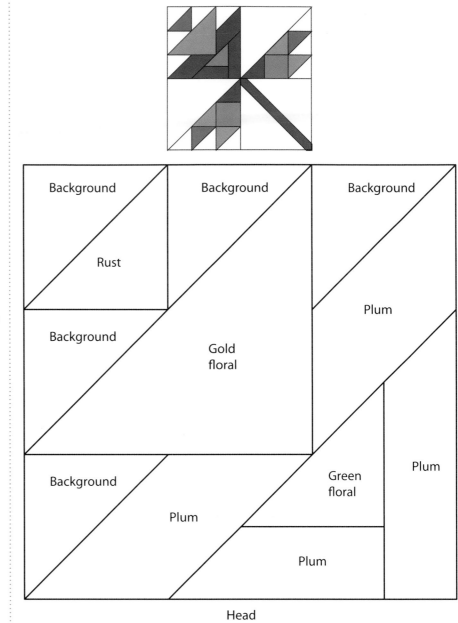

Paper piecing pattern for head

3. Cut fabric strips for sewing. I allow plenty of wiggle room because it makes piecing much easier, and in the long run, doesn't use that much more fabric. I add 1" to the finished width of the piece and 1½" to the length, which allows for the ¼" seam allowance for the finished block, in addition to the wiggle room. I tend to cut my fabrics as I piece. This allows me to use my fabric scraps, and it makes it much easier to change my mind about colors and fabrics.

4. Place the fabric for piece 1 on the pattern. Pin paper and fabric together once in the middle.

![tip icon] *tip*

I think the easiest way to pin them together is to place the fabric right side down on a table, and then place the pattern right side up on the fabric. You can easily check that the fabric has been placed properly by holding the pattern up to a light source. Be sure that at least ¼" of fabric extends beyond all edges.

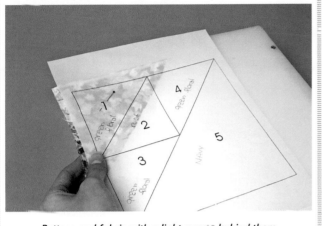

Pattern and fabric with a light source behind them

5. With the right side of the pattern up, place a pin at each corner of the stitching line for pieces 1 and 2.

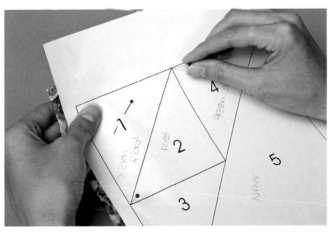

Pattern with pins at the pattern's corners

6. Flip the pattern over—fabric, pins, and all—and place the fabric for piece 2 over the pins, allowing at least a ¼" seam allowance. Pin piece 2 into place.

Two pinned fabrics

7. Sew along the printed line of the pattern. Remove the pins as you go.

8. Press the seam. This is very important! Don't skip this step and wait until you have a lot of pieces sewn on the pattern. The finished block will have much crisper points and seams if you press after every seam has been sewn.

9. Repeat Steps 5 through 8 until the entire block has been pieced. Don't forget to extend the fabric at least ¼" over the outside edge of the pattern. This will become the block's seam allowance

10. Once the final piece has been sewn in place, press the block, and trim to a ¼" seam allowance around the outside edge.

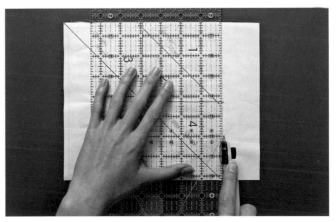

Trim piece with ruler and rotary cutter.

11. Carefully remove the paper by first creasing along the paper's stitching line and then gently tearing the paper away.

HOW WILL I KNOW IF A PATTERN CAN BE PAPER PIECED?

The simple answer is to follow the paths of the seams. First, decide which pieces share common seams.

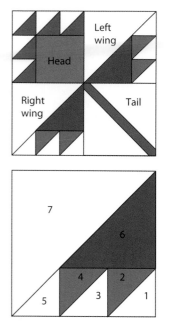

Which pattern pieces share common seams?

The small triangles in this wing section (1, 2, 3, 4, and 5; the numbers refer to the piecing order) share a common seam with the larger piece 6. The small triangles are sewn first. The small triangles and piece 6 share a common seam with piece 7. Sew piece 6 to the smaller triangle section, and then sew the entire section to piece 7.

MODIFIED PAPER PIECING

Sometimes it's impossible to sew the pieces of an entire block together in one section. The way around this problem is to sew the block in sections.

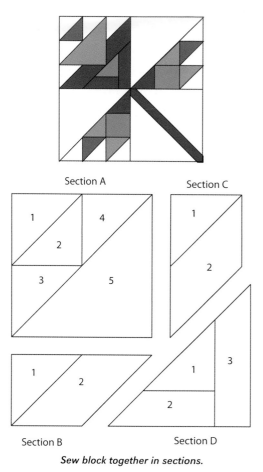

Sew block together in sections.

This example builds the block in four sewn sections. Once a section is sewn, it is pressed and trimmed to a ¼" seam allowance. The paper is removed, and the sections are sewn together. Don't forget to carefully match the seams where necessary.

Sometimes it's better to paper piece some parts of a motif and regularly piece other parts, such as places where four squares meet, or in the head section of Block 1.

The exception comes if the block is very small. Fabric stretches a bit and is quite forgiving on a large scale, but as the size of the piece diminishes, so does the fabric's flexibility. While a ¼" seam allowance is always a must, it is imperative that it's *exact* when the pieces are very small. Because of this, you might want to paper piece for the sake of accuracy. So Section A would be traditionally pieced, and Sections B and C would be paper pieced.

Calculating Fabric

Of course, we always want to know how much fabric we need. But I'm not sure there is actually a good answer. The obvious answer is to add up all the pieces using a particular fabric, plot how many will fit into 40 linear inches—the general width of cotton fabric after washing—and calculate the sizes from there. If you're paper piecing, don't be alarmed if the final fabric amount is more than that of traditional piecing. This is normal because of the wiggle room allowance.

All of the fabric amounts given for the quilts in this book are based on traditional piecing. If you template piece, the amounts will remain the same. If you paper piece, you will need more fabric than is suggested.

Choosing Fabric

I like to use a lot of different fabrics in a quilt. I'm lucky because I have quite an extensive fabric stash. So when I quilt, I think more in terms of "I will need × number of pieces in a particular color range," and then go from there. Because I cut and piece as I go in my quilting, the colors may change a bit as the quilt piecing progresses. This brings me to the tale of the green-and-blue quilt.

Wisteria Arbor was supposed to be green and blue. (See page 53.) I thought the center medallions would be predominantly blue, the Dragonfly motif would be a mix of greens, and the Flying Geese would be dark red. I sorted my fabrics and scrap stash and started with the greens. I didn't have much mint green, but I had a lot of light yellow-green. I'm flexible, and I like yellow-green. Next, I went to the reds. Well, that was the plan, but I accidentally opened the violet bin instead and got sucked in by the red-violet fabrics. Okay, another change of plans. The quilt would now be yellow-green, red-violet, and blue-green. And that's when I discovered that I didn't have enough blue-green to complete the quilt, even when I mixed fabrics. But I did have a lot of a fabric with violet and green motifs on a white background.

The point is to be flexible. Start with one section of the quilt, and let your color decisions change and grow with the quilt. As for making do with what you have, if what you have doesn't work for your quilt, don't use it. Change your plans!

repeating the block

Traditionally, the Dragonfly block would have been repeated by alternating it with a plain block, or by adding sashing between rotated blocks. Both options create beautiful quilts. There are many other ways to repeat this fascinating block, such as alternating positive and negative squares, or turning the blocks on point.

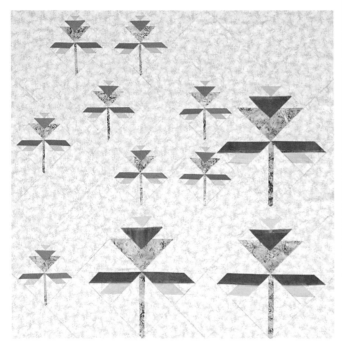

Dragonfly block repeated in different sizes.

These time-honored ways of repeating a block are popular for a reason. You can't go wrong! It's pretty hard to make an ugly quilt using these methods. But there are some less conventional ways of repeating a block that absolutely fascinate me.

One of my favorite ways to repeat the block is to change the size of it within the quilt. As you can well imagine, this allows for myriad variations.

Mirroring the Block

If you repeat the block with its mirror image, secondary patterns emerge. It's not really mirrored but only rotated, because the block is symmetrical on one axis. This is easiest to see if you turn the block on point.

An axis line is drawn through the Dragonfly block to show mirror image.

What is on the left side of the vertical axis is an exact mirror image of what is on the right side. This is true of all of the Dragonfly blocks. Because of this symmetry, rotating the block 90°, then 180°, then 270° will give the effect of four mirrored blocks. Placing different corners of the block in the center will generate different designs.

In this example of Block 6, the Dragonfly heads point outward.

In this example of Block 2, the two heads and two tails point toward each other and outward.

In this example of Block 4, the two heads and two tails point toward each other and outward.

In this example of Block 5, the Dragonfly heads point inward.

Because mirroring the block produces such different effects, I have found it handy to use an arrow to indicate the direction of the Dragonfly motif. The head of the arrow corresponds to the head of the Dragonfly. The tail corresponds to the tail.

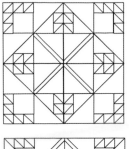
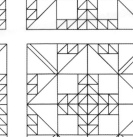

Original Block blanks

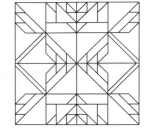
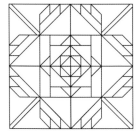
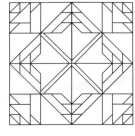
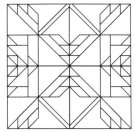

Block 3 blanks

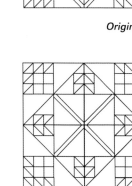
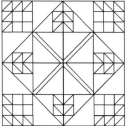
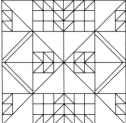
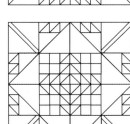

Block 1 blanks

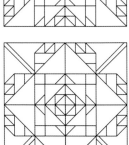
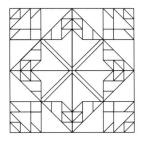
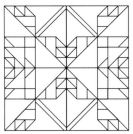

Block 4 blanks

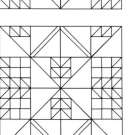
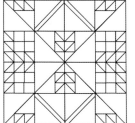
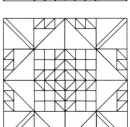

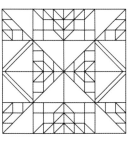
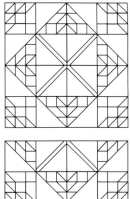
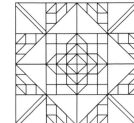

Block 2 blanks

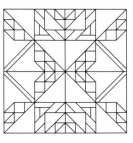
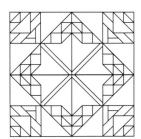
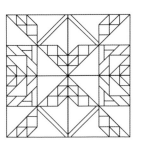
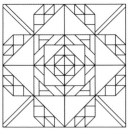

Block 5 blanks

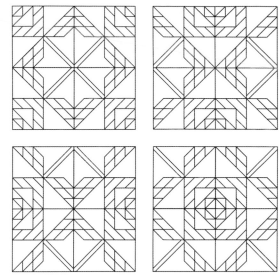

Block 6 blanks

Adding Color to the Block

You can use a couple of methods to add color to the design. You can design the block, color and all, mirror it however you choose, and then see what sort of design you get. Serendipity is a marvelous thing, and 99 times out of 100, you will love the results. Or you can decide on the way you want to mirror the block and then add the colors to bring out the design you want to create. If you choose this option, be sure to remember that each block's background doesn't necessarily have to be the same when blocks are repeated.

Repeating the Block to Form New Motifs

There are still more possibilities. You can combine the different ways of mirroring the block to create new patterns. Each block and each mirroring variation will create new secondary and tertiary designs. This is how the quilts in this book were designed.

The simplest way to create new motifs is to start with four mirrored blocks. Then twelve more blocks can surround them. For example, the sixteen blocks can be all mirrored facing outward, and a star will appear in the design (highlighted in light violet below). It doesn't matter which block you use, because the star motif is formed by the "blank" wing and tail sections.

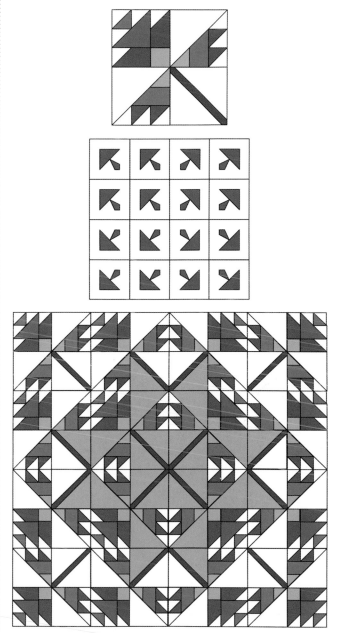

How you use color will determine what your secondary patterns will be. Here, a star appears in the design.

A tertiary design of Flying Geese is also present (highlighted in light orange below). But those aren't the only designs possible. You can also see squares and diamonds.

At this point, you are now seeing secondary and tertiary designs that I haven't mentioned. Here is a chance for you to find your own.

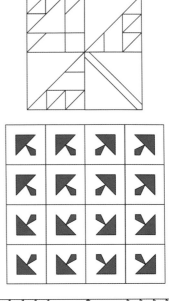

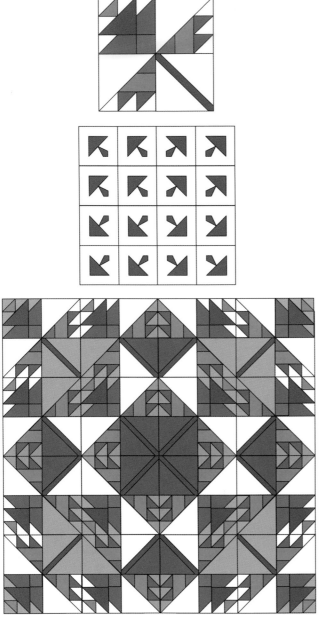

Flying geese, squares, and diamonds can also appear.

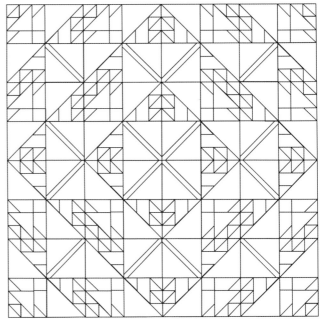

What do you see? Stars, diamonds, or a V?
Plan your own secondary patterns.

What happens if the Dragonfly motifs are mirrored so that they all face inward?

Or, they can face a combination of directions.

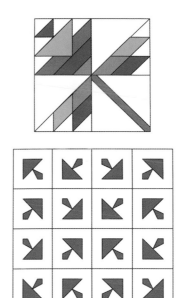

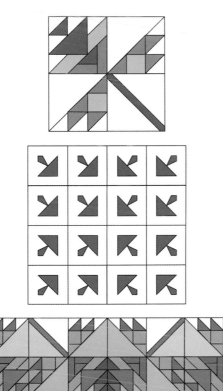

Mirrored Dragonfly motifs face inward.

Turn the blocks in a combination of both directions for yet another variation.

I have purposely left much of this illustration blank, so you might want to take a moment to fill in the secondary and tertiary designs. The possibilities seem endless, and the secondary and tertiary designs change with each variation. This is how each of the quilt designs was devised.

Isolating and Repeating a Portion of the Pattern

By now I'm sure you realize that when mirrored, the head motif creates a different design than the tail motif. Sometimes you may just want to repeat the head motif.

An inward-facing head block

An outward-facing head block

Dragonfly heads face outward and toward each other.

Because the head is different in all of the Dragonfly blocks, the design will be different for each block. Additionally, within each block different secondary and tertiary patterns will form, and color placement will bring them out or disguise them.

Actually, any section of the Dragonfly block can be repeated. Below are examples of what happens when only the right wing from Block 4 is repeated.

The right wing has been rotated around its large "background" triangle.

The right wing has been rotated to form a Pinwheel design.

The large background blocks of the right wing form a Pinwheel.

The rotated right wing blocks form a center diamond.

Don't forget that the wing blocks in each Dragonfly block variation are different and will create a different illusion when repeated.

What happens if both wings are repeated? New designs form.

Block 3's left and right wings are repeated with the wing tips touching.

Block 3's left and right wings are repeated with the wing tips pointing outward.

Again, the different Dragonfly blocks have different wings, and each will create a distinctive design. And don't forget that you can change their orientation.

What would happen if the background triangle of the wing block was replaced with another wing motif? You'd get a double wing.

In these examples, Block 6's wing can be paired with its reverse.

Single left wing block

Reversed double wing block

This reversed double wing can then be repeated.

Repeated double wing block

In another example, a left and right wing can be paired to form a mirrored double wing.

Mirrored double wing from Block 1

And, of course, the double wings can be mirrored. The direction of the wing before mirroring will produce an entirely different image.

Block 4 wing with the tips pointing outward

Block 4 wing with the tips pointing inward. Note the "flying geese."

Is there more? Sure. Sashing can be placed between the double wing blocks.

Block 3: Wing with sashing and a center square

It is important to remember that because each block has a different wing, the pattern that it creates when doubled and mirrored will be unique.

Replacing a Portion of the Motif

Believe it or not, there's more you can do to modify the Dragonfly motif. A portion of the block, such as the tail, can be eliminated and then replaced with another part of the block, such as the head. Or the tail can be replaced with a half-sized Dragonfly block. This new block can then be mirrored.

Half-sized Dragonfly blocks replace tail.

This is how *Lilypad* was designed on page 58. Replacement can be done with any part of the block. Because each block is different, the design that results will be different.

One of my favorite effects is doubled wings and tails. This is prominent in *Dragonfly Moon* on page 71.

Dragonfly Block 4 with double wings and tails

These blocks can then be mirrored and repeated.

Dragonfly wing from Block 4 with tails meeting in the center

Dragonfly wing from Block 1 with tails forming a center diamond

Many of the quilts in this book have been designed using this technique. Different blocks will create different designs. Is it any wonder I find this block so fascinating?

planning the quilt

Determining Quilt Size

As I mentioned before, each of the Dragonfly quilt blocks can be divided by 6. It's basically a four patch, and each individual patch can be subdivided into 9 squares, for a total of 36 squares in a 6-by-6 patch.

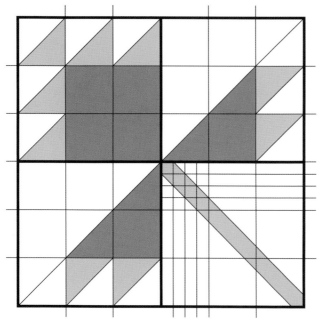

Once again, see how the Dragonfly block can be divided for ease in design options.

Whatever the final size of your quilt (minus sashing) turns out to be, if it is divisible by six, you're in luck! And this will work whether you're using centimeters or inches.

But what do you do if your finished size isn't easily divisible by 6? For example, you have determined that your final quilt size should be about 74″ square, or 188 cm. And you have decided that you would like the quilt to be six blocks across. If you divide 74″ by 6, you will see that each block needs to be 12.33333″, or 31.33 cm. Both of these measurements are impractical. So you have two choices:

1. Make each block 12¼″. Your quilt's finished size would be 73½″.

2. Make each block 12½″. Your finished quilt would be 75″.

Everyone is happy, right? Well, not exactly. If you decide to go with the first choice, you'll find that the finished size of each small square in the block is 2¹⁄₂₄″ (each of the four patches would be 6⅛″). This means that the cutting size of each small triangle is 2¹¹⁄₁₂″. This is not a practical measurement to be using, unless you're paper piecing. If you decide to go with the second choice, you will discover that the finished size for each small triangle would be 2½″. Again, this isn't a practical measurement to use. Trust me, this example doesn't work out using centimeters either.

There is a solution. Remember the block size chart in Chapter 2 on page 18? Make a quilt size chart using these sizes. Check out the chart, and use the block size that is closest to the size you want. For example, according to the chart, there is a 12″ block. Six blocks, each 12″ by 12″, would make a 72″ quilt, which for many quilters is close enough. Not close enough for you? Add a 1″ border around the entire quilt. It's quite attractive, and your quilt is now exactly 74″.

Quilt Layout

As you saw in Chapter 3, the blocks' orientation is important, but it is only one part of the quilt's design. Quilt layout—the way that the pieced blocks are placed in the quilt—is equally important. The first thing to consider is the number of blocks in the quilt. The basic question here is: do you want an even number of blocks or an odd number?

If you are mirroring the block to create secondary motifs, you will use an even number of blocks. Look carefully at the following drawn quilts. Each quilt is four blocks wide by six blocks tall. One mirrors the Dragonfly motif at the tail blocks, and the other at the head.

These two quilts use the same blocks with a different placement for a completely different look.

It's the same block, but the effect is quite different. You will need to keep this in mind when planning the layout of your quilt. Don't forget that the secondary patterns each layout creates will be different.

What if a quilt that is five blocks wide and five blocks tall is the perfect size, but you want to maintain the symmetrical feel? Mirroring the block may not be the answer.

This quilt looks a bit odd and unbalanced. Even the contrasting binding isn't helping.

Instead, you might want to alternate the Dragonfly block with a plain block, as in my version of the original quilt, found in Chapter 1 on page 7.

This is a very traditional quilt layout, and the reason it is so popular is that it never fails to create a beautiful quilt. Don't forget that the plain blocks don't necessarily have to be the same color as the Dragonfly block's background. Plain blocks can also be used to intensify a secondary image, as in *Dragonfly in the Sun* on page 80. Or, they can be used to elongate a quilt without destroying the symmetrical feel, as is shown in *Oasis* on page 60. A portion of the Dragonfly motif—in this case, a head—can be placed within the plain block and also as a center block.

There's still more. How about some double wings along with the plain blocks? Don't forget that the filler blocks, plain or otherwise, don't necessarily have to be the same size as the Dragonfly block. *Oasis* on page 60 uses plain half blocks to vertically elongate the quilt without destroying the symmetrical feel.

What about sashing? Usually sashing is a plain spacer between blocks, but it doesn't have to be. A small motif from the Dragonfly block can be repeated and flanked by plain strips to form a striking sashing.

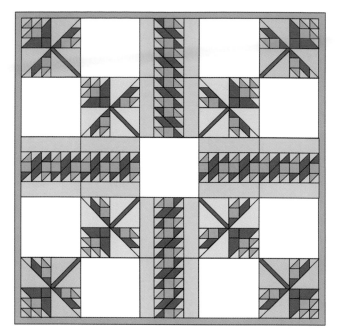

Double wings form a sashing, which dresses up a simple arrangement of Dragonfly blocks.

What about using Flying Geese blocks? I'm sure that at this point, you have plenty of ideas. Here's a chance for you to fill in the blanks with your own ideas.

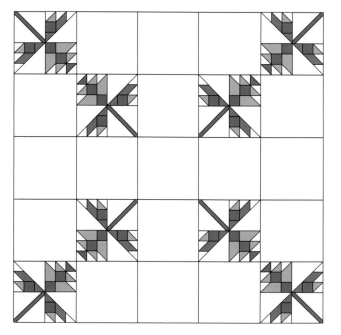

Fill in your own motifs in the plain blocks.

Don't forget that the Dragonfly block can be turned on point. *Midsummer's Day Dance* on page 77 shows this best. Actually, an entire quilt can be made using this technique.

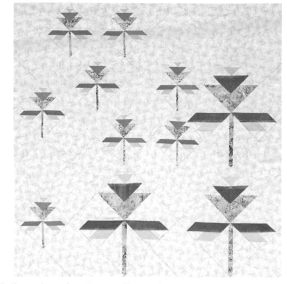

Quilt top based on Dragonfly motifs in two sizes, turned on point

It's a lot to think about. Exciting, isn't it?

Planning Borders

Some folks insist that every quilt should have a border. Some say just the opposite. I prefer to tackle the question on a quilt-by-quilt basis.

Border strips are a great way to adjust the size of your quilt. They can also be incorporated into the quilt as part of the design. A single strip can really make a quilt dance and sing, especially if plain corner blocks are used, such as in *Loop De Loop*, page 87. Two or three strips of fabric from the quilt can form a very attractive border, as you can see in *Dragonfly Moon* on page 71 and *Midsummer's Day Dance* on page 77.

The strips do not need to be the same size. A border made of a wider background fabric strip, set off by smaller strips, can be a perfect place for decorative stitching, as shown in *Lilypad* on page 58.

One of my favorite kinds of borders uses sashing between the quilt body and the border, as in *Spring Fling* on page 66. Judicious color placement can create the illusion of the interior motif expanding into the border, which is an effect I particularly like, as in *Dragonfly in the Sun* on page 80.

Integrating Quilting into the Quilt Design

Your top is made, and it's wonderful. It's time to think about the quilting. This is where many quilts fall apart, at least visually. Quilting should be more than just a way to hold the quilt layers together; it should be an integral part of the quilt design. Just because a quilt motif is beautiful doesn't mean that it's the right motif for your quilt. The quilted motif should complement the block motif, and it should be placed appropriately within the motif.

Many excellent books deal with this topic. But I would also like to make a few points. Quilts that have a busy overall pattern need simple quilting, like that found in *Sparkling Spring Afternoon* on page 50. Also, small decorative machine stitches make great quilting stitches. I find they are particularly effective when a contrasting thread is used on a plain background as in *Wisteria Arbor* on page 53 and *Oasis* on page 60.

Also, large areas with a plain fabric are the perfect place for stitched decorative motifs, as in *Lilypad* on page 58. These are also the perfect places for stippled backgrounds and decorative motifs, like those used in *Dragonfly in the Sun* on page 80.

Beading is also a finishing touch that adds so much to the quilt, as in *Spring Fling* on page 66.

Beading detail on velveteen from **Spring Fling**

Don't forget that a beautiful quilt deserves a beautiful quilt batting. You can find many lovely quilt battings on the market. Different types of batting require different amounts of stitching and have different degrees of loft. Be sure to choose one that will give you the loft, warmth, and stitch ease that you desire.

Finally, and this is a very important consideration for me, a beautiful quilt needs beautiful quilting thread. This is not the place to skimp. I use variegated threads and metallic threads exclusively. Remember, quilting is more than just a way to hold the layers together. It is an integral part of the quilt design!

Machine decorative stitches accentuate triangles in **All Aflutter** *(page 63).*

choosing the fabrics

Tips on Mixing Fabrics

I'm never sure what part I like best about making a quilt—the process of designing it, making it, or picking out the fabric—but I'm leaning toward the fabric. There's something about being surrounded by all that wonderful color, visual texture, and tactile texture. This is because I don't just use cotton fabrics. I love silk and velveteen, and use them on a regular basis in my quilts.

Cotton

I love quilting with cotton fabric. It's user-friendly, has a flat, smooth surface, is easily washed and dried, and holds its shape well in a quilt. It comes in myriad colors and prints—batiks, florals, geometric patterns, solid colors, and more. It's lightweight, which is important in a quilt. When printed, it has a right and a wrong side, which allows a quilter the option of using both sides for value changes. Batiks have no right or wrong side, and mirror images can be obtained by simply flipping the fabric over.

Cotton is easy to clean. You just throw it in the washer and dryer. It's also easily ironed and withstands a fairly high iron temperature (400° F), which allows you to use steam, a great option for removing wrinkles. Cotton usually doesn't fray easily.

Cotton fabric is slightly directional and stretches a bit more on the width of grain than on the length of grain, which is why quilters are encouraged to use the length of grain for sashing and binding. It stretches even more on the diagonal, which can be good or bad, depending on your perspective. It definitely makes life interesting when two diagonal fabric pieces are sewn. We quilters have learned some tricks to deal with that problem, such as using an even-feed or walking foot, pinning often, and not pulling on the fabric during sewing. I'm sure you can think of a few more tips that I've forgotten.

Quilters who do a lot of appliqué love the fact that cotton has a fair amount of diagonal stretch. In fact, they rely on it. No wonder cotton fabric is a staple for all quilters! Some quilters spend a lifetime only using cotton fabric, and they remain quite happy and content.

However, cotton doesn't do one thing that I really like. It doesn't shine. Yes, I know that there is polished cotton, but the effect will disappear with washing. I'm talking about a permanent sheen.

Silk

Silk comes in many varieties, depending on the type of silkworm it is harvested from and the way the thread is manufactured and woven. I'm partial to 100% silk Habotai, which is a classic kimono-quality silk. It has an amazing sheen and can be machine washed and dried. The rich, vibrant colors are unparalleled.

Habotai means "soft as down" in Japanese.

Unfortunately, this amazing fabric also has a downside, at least in some quilting circumstances. It has such amazing drape and is so slinky that it doesn't hold its shape well. It also stretches when it's wet, so you can't steam or spritz it to remove wrinkles. It needs to be ironed with a relatively cool iron (300° F). If the iron is too hot, it will drag and distort the fabric, or worse yet, burn it.

This fabric is also difficult to cut. A pair of very sharp scissors or a new rotary cutting blade must be used, and it doesn't stay well on a cutting mat. Trust me, it's tough to cut something that tries to run away or won't hold still to an exact size. And if that isn't bad enough, silk can be difficult to sew if your needle isn't very sharp. You have to pin silk—a lot. And you really need to pay attention when sewing; it likes to escape from under the presser foot.

So why does anyone bother with this fabric? Because it's amazingly beautiful, and if it's fused to a fine interfacing, it's as easy to work with as cotton.

Fusing Silk

Use the lightest possible fusible web that you can find, and make sure that it will fuse at a low iron temperature. First, iron your silk. Then place the fusible web sticky side up on your ironing board. Place the silk on top of the web, and press with an up-and-down motion. Do not iron back and forth, or the web and the silk will shift, and the silk will be permanently wrinkled. Of course, you might like the wrinkled effect.

Fused silk is a stable fabric that is close to the same weight as most quilting cottons. You can sew it with cotton thread, and it will hold its shape. It's easily cut and doesn't try to escape when you sew it. Just don't forget that it is silk and must be ironed with a cool iron. When you use it with cotton fabric in a quilt, I suggest that you keep the iron on a silk setting. As long as the cotton fabric has been pressed very well before cutting, I don't find that the cooler iron setting is a problem when pressing the seams where the silk and cotton are joined.

Fused silk is very easy to quilt, and any quilting technique or stitch that you use for cotton can be used for silk. Just make sure that your needle is very sharp. Believe it or not, I just use a regular needle, but I do put in a new needle before I begin sewing the silk. Be careful when pinning or basting the quilt layers together. If at all possible, try not to pin on silk fabric because the pins may leave tiny holes behind. If you baste your layers together, I would suggest using a rayon or silk thread. Cotton or poly-wrapped cotton thread can leave pieces of fuzz behind. Most of all, try really hard not to make mistakes that need to be ripped out. Even fused silk is not that forgiving!

Velveteen

If silk is fine and gossamer, velveteen is just the opposite. It is a fairly heavy fabric.

It absorbs and reflects light simultaneously, which gives it an amazing visual depth and texture. And it feels great! Who wouldn't want to snuggle in a quilt with velveteen in it?

Various velveteens

Velveteen has a nap that runs along the lengthwise grain of the fabric. It's easy to feel when you rub your hand over the fabric. One direction will be smooth, and the other will be rough. It's the nap's direction that affects the light's reflection, so know that the color will be slightly different when viewed at different angles.

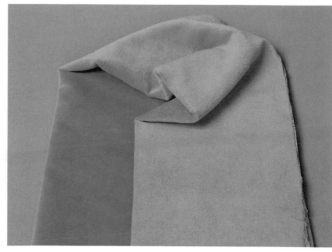

Light reflecting differently off of the same velveteen

My favorite velveteen is made from 100% cotton, so it can be ironed with a hot iron. Because of its weight, it drapes less than regular cotton. It also has more stretch along its width than regular cotton and almost no stretch along the fabric grain's length. It is quite stretchy on the diagonal bias.

So does it have any downside? Oh yeah. It frays like crazy. If you forget to lower the presser-foot pressure while sewing, it will distort the fabric, especially when you're sewing on the widthwise grain or bias. Velveteen also attracts lint and sewing debris. But all of these problems can be solved.

1. Wash the fabric before sewing. I wash all of my quilting fabric first, but with velveteen, it's imperative. Just throw it in the washing machine and dryer on the normal or cotton setting. This will allow it to shrink a bit, tightening the spaces between the threads. You'll get gobs of fuzz in the lint basket, but don't let that worry you. Your velveteen will become quite docile and will be much less prone to fraying. However, all bets are off if you have to rip out a seam. The key is to handle cut velveteen pieces as little as possible.

2. Reduce the pressure on the presser foot when sewing, and pin often. Actually, when sewing with cotton and velveteen in the same quilt, you may find it necessary to change the foot pressure midstream, less for all velvet sections, more for all cotton sections. This isn't much of a chore to do as long as you remember to do it. An even-feed or walking foot will make your life so much easier!

3. Use a loop of masking tape to remove lint and stray threads.

4. When sewing cotton and velveteen together, or fused silk and velveteen, be aware that the lighter fabric will migrate in the direction of the velveteen's nap. This will throw your ¼" seam off. Pinning the two pieces together every inch or so should alleviate the problem. Everything will then stay put as you sew it.

5. Pin either side of the seam intersections. Because of the thickness variation between velveteen and cotton, or velveteen and silk, you will need to pin on either side of seam intersections instead of at the intersection.

6. A perfect ¼" seam allowance will not work with velveteen. You'll find that your finished block measurements will be off. This is because the thickness of the velveteen causes the seams to take up space. The solution is to use a seam allowance that is a couple of threads *less* than ¼".

Using different fabrics in a quilt isn't hard once you understand each fabric. The results are so rewarding that it's really worth the time it takes to learn their idiosyncrasies.

*Velveteen provides visual depth in **Spring Fling** (page 66).*

Suzie's Sew-As-You-Go Quilting Method

Have you ever noticed that some quilts sing and dance, while others just sit there? I'm convinced the reason is that some quilters listen to the quilt as it is being constructed, and some don't. It might sound strange, but a quilt will tell you what it needs to be fabulous.

I never cut all of my fabric pieces for the entire quilt prior to construction. I find that doing this limits my design options, because I'm less likely to make changes once the pieces are cut. I still carefully plan my quilts. I'm just very willing to make revisions as the quilt progresses.

I don't have a design wall. For that matter, I don't have a quilting studio. I wish I did, but I don't, and that's life. What I do have is a good imagination and the experience to realize that careful planning is the key to my quilting success. By careful planning, I don't mean that I plan down to the last detail. Instead, I make a solid plan that gives me options for modifications. Here are some of my tips for starting a quilt:

1. Start with your quilt design. I carefully preplan the block size, orientation, color pathways, and border. This plan doesn't change. It is the one constant in the quilt.

2. Decide on the main color you want to use in the quilt. I sort my fabrics into six groups: reds, oranges, yellows, greens, blues, and violets. Some colors will jump the boundaries of their color group depending on the surrounding colors. In color theory terms, this is called simultaneous contrast. But the general groupings give me a place to start. My fabric stash contains hand-painted fabrics, batiks, florals, geometrics, and more. In other words, I have a wide visual range of fabrics. Almost by definition, these fabrics contain more than one color, so when I sort them, I sort by the most prevalent color. Additionally, I have a nifty stash of solid-colored velveteen and silk fabrics. I don't generally use solids in my quilts because I feel that visually, they leave a flat spot. But velveteens and silks are different. Silks are shiny, and velveteens simultaneously reflect and absorb light. Together they give a quilt a textural depth that isn't possible when cotton alone is used.

I decide on a main color for my quilt, like blue, and grab all of the fabrics that fall within that category, being careful to include light, medium, and dark forms of the color. Contrast is a very important component of a successful quilt. When it comes to fabric, I am a believer in "more is better," so my stash is fairly extensive. Additionally, I suffer from pack-rat syndrome and hate to throw away little fabric pieces. Small pieces come in very handy when I need just a spark of color.

3. Choose a second and third color for your quilt, and pull those fabrics. I place all of the fabrics out on my bed, because it's a nice, large, flat surface, and then I start eliminating. Some fabrics may be too bright or too dull for what I have in mind, or some might move things in a color direction that I may not wish to go. If they're close, I might set them aside for reconsideration, but usually I save them for another quilt. When I'm done, I have a fairly large pile of potential fabrics. No matter how beautiful the fabric is, close is not good enough. If it isn't perfect, I set it aside.

I then sort my potential fabrics from dark to light within each color group. Because I work from a black, white, and gray quilt pattern, value (the lightness or darkness of a fabric) becomes one of the most important components in the quilt. This is a good time to check that all of the chosen fabrics are compatible, and that you have a good mix of lights, mediums, and darks within each color group.

Then I start sewing, which, if you've been reading this book from the beginning, I'm sure you're ready to do. Pick an idea that has been previously discussed, or pick one of the following quilts, and go for it! Most of all, **have fun**!

All of the fabric amounts given in the quilt instructions are for conventionally pieced or template-pieced blocks. Paper pieced blocks will require more fabric. Please see Calculating Fabric on page 29.

QUILT DESIGNS

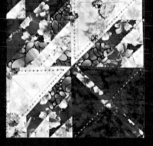

sparkling spring afternoon

Quilt size: 78˝ × 78˝
Finished block sizes: 18˝ × 18˝, 9˝ × 9˝

This quilt uses Dragonfly Block 1. It requires only four fabrics, each of which has the feel of a hand-painted fabric. This creates a quilt that is like a painting, with individual components of the blocks blending together. Also, some isolated motifs were fussy cut and then rotated in the large head blocks. The side blocks are composed of a modified head, two tails, and a double wing.

Make the blocks following the Dragonfly Block 1 piecing order on page 20.

Materials

- Dark green: 1⅞ yards
- Dark green leaf: 1¼ yards
- Medium green/pink: 1¾ yards
- Light pink/green floral: 3¾ yards (including border)
- Binding: ¾ yard
- Backing: 4¾ yards
- Batting: 82˝ × 82˝

CENTER BLOCK

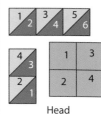

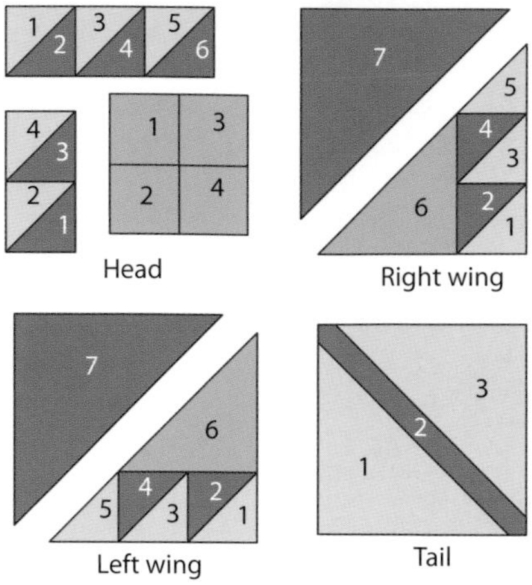

Head

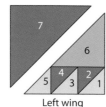

Right wing

Left wing

Tail

Finished size: 18˝ × 18˝
Make 4 blocks.

DARK GREEN

1. Cut 4 squares 9⅞˝ × 9⅞˝; cut in half diagonally.

2. Cut 18 squares 3⅞˝ × 3⅞˝; cut in half diagonally.

3. Cut 4 rectangles 1½˝ × 13½˝.

MEDIUM GREEN/PINK

1. Cut 4 squares 6⅞˝ × 6⅞˝; cut in half diagonally.

2. Cut 16 squares 3½˝ × 3½˝, with a motif isolated in the center of each. Rotate the squares before piecing to create the desired effect.

Detail with rotated, fussy-cut squares

LIGHT PINK/GREEN FLORAL

1. Cut 4 squares 9⅛″ × 9⅛″; cut in half diagonally.

2. Cut 22 squares 3⅞″ × 3⅞″; cut in half diagonally.

SIDE BLOCK A

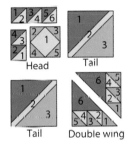

Head   Tail

Tail   Double wing

Finished size: 9″ × 9″
Make 8 blocks.

DARK GREEN

1. Cut 8 squares 3⅞″ × 3⅞″; cut in half diagonally.

2. Cut 8 squares 5″ × 5″; cut in half diagonally.

3. Cut 20 squares 2⅜″ × 2⅜″; cut in half diagonally.

DARK GREEN LEAF

Cut 24 squares 2⅜″ × 2⅜″; cut in half diagonally.

MEDIUM GREEN/PINK

1. Cut 8 squares 5″ × 5″; cut in half diagonally.

2. Cut 16 squares 2⅜″ × 2⅜″; cut in half diagonally.

LIGHT PINK/GREEN FLORAL

1. Cut 8 squares 2⅝″ × 2⅝″.

2. Cut 36 squares 2⅜″ × 2⅜″; cut in half diagonally.

3. Cut 16 rectangles 1″ × 7⅛″.

SIDE BLOCK B

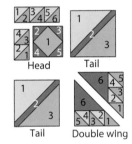

Head   Tail

Tail   Double wing

Finished size: 9″ × 9″
Make 24 blocks.

DARK GREEN

1. Cut 24 squares 3⅞″ × 3⅞″; cut in half diagonally.

2. Cut 48 squares 2⅜″ × 2⅜″; cut in half diagonally.

3. Cut 48 rectangles 1″ × 7⅛″.

DARK GREEN LEAF

Cut 132 squares 2⅜″ × 2⅜″; cut in half diagonally.

MEDIUM GREEN/PINK

1. Cut 24 squares 5″ × 5″.

2. Cut 24 squares 2⅝″ × 2⅝″; cut in half diagonally.

LIGHT PINK/GREEN FLORAL

1. Cut 24 squares 5″ × 5″; cut in half diagonally.

2. Cut 108 squares 2⅜″ × 2⅜″; cut in half diagonally.

CORNER BLOCK

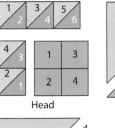

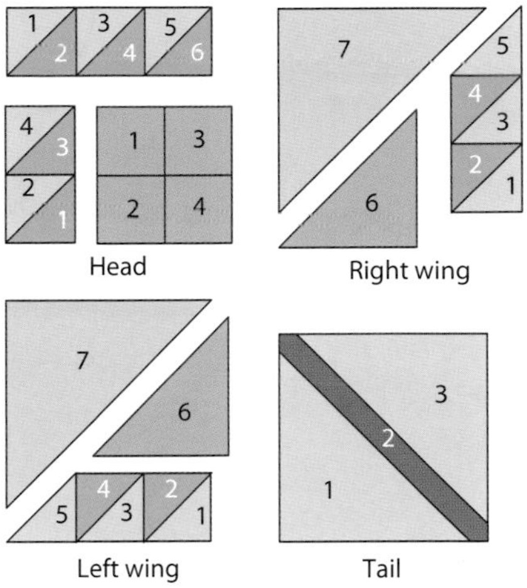

Head   Right wing

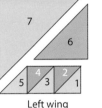

Left wing   Tail

Finished size: 18″ × 18″
Make 4 blocks.

DARK GREEN

Cut 4 rectangles 1½″ × 13½″.

DARK GREEN LEAF

Cut 18 squares 3⅞″ × 3⅞″; cut in half diagonally.

MEDIUM GREEN/PINK

1. Cut 4 squares 6⅞″ × 6⅞″; cut in half diagonally.

2. Cut 16 squares 3½″ × 3½″, with a motif isolated in the center of each. Rotate the squares before piecing.

LIGHT PINK/GREEN FLORAL

1. Cut 4 squares 9⅛″ × 9⅛″; cut in half diagonally.

2. Cut 4 squares 9⅞″ × 9⅞″; cut in half diagonally.

3. Cut 22 squares 3⅞″ × 3⅞″; cut in half diagonally.

Quilt Construction

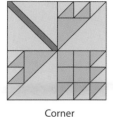
Corner

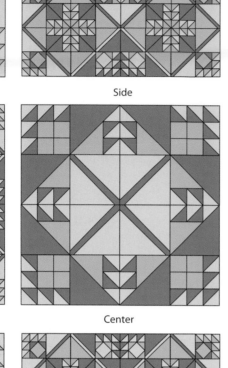
Side

Corner

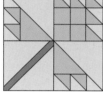
Side

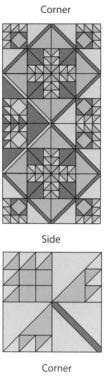
Center

Side

Corner

Side

Corner

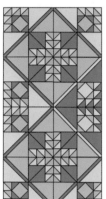

Assembly diagram

Press carefully as each piece is sewn.

1. Sew the 4 center blocks together. Be sure the head section of each block is pointing outward, and the double wing section is pointing inward. Press carefully.

2. Arrange and sew the side blocks together, forming 4 rectangles.

3. Sew the center section, side sections, and corner blocks into 3 rows.

4. Sew the rows together.

5. Make 2 border strips 3½" × 72½" of light pink floral. Sew to the sides of the quilt.

6. Make 2 border strips 3½" × 78½" of light pink floral. Sew to the top and bottom of the quilt.

Quilting

Although some decorative stitches have been used, the quilting has been purposely kept simple to avoid interrupting the allover effect of the fabric blending. Straight and wavy lines were mostly used.

wisteria arbor

Quilt size: 81˝ × 108˝
Finished block sizes: 6¾˝ × 6¾˝, 13½˝ × 13½˝

This quilt uses Dragonfly Block 3. It is made from three large blocks, each containing multiple Dragonfly blocks. The large corner and center blocks each contain sixteen small Dragonfly blocks. The eight large side blocks contain four large Dragonfly blocks, each measuring 13½˝ × 13½˝.

Because the parallelograms are mirror images in the block, cut half of the pieces angled right and half angled left. Pay attention to the diagram for the correct angles for the trapezoid pieces. Make the blocks following the Dragonfly Block 3 piecing order on page 21.

Materials

- ■ Light turquoise floral: 1¼ yards
- ■ Dark blue: 3 yards
- ■ Turquoise: ¾ yard
- ■ Violet/green leaves: 1¼ yards
- ■ Medium green: 2¼ yards
- ■ Medium violet: ¾ yard
- ■ White: 3¾ yards
- ■ Violet/green floral: 2½ yards
- ■ Dark violet: ¼ yard
- ■ Dark green: 1 yard
- ■ Binding: ⅞ yard
- ■ Backing: 7¼ yards (pieced widthwise)
- ■ Batting: 85˝ × 112˝

Large Center Block
Each large center block is composed of 16 smaller 6¾˝ square Dragonfly blocks.

SMALL CENTER BLOCK

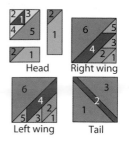

Head Right wing
Left wing Tail

Finished size: 6¾″ × 6¾″
Make 8 blocks.

LIGHT TURQUOISE FLORAL

Cut 12 squares 2″ × 2″; cut in half diagonally.

DARK BLUE

1. Cut 4 squares 2″ × 2″; cut in half diagonally.

2. Cut 16 parallelograms 1¼″ × 5¼″.

3. Cut 8 rectangles ⅞″ × 5½″.

TURQUOISE

1. Cut 4 squares 3⅛″ × 3⅛″; cut in half diagonally.

2. Cut 16 parallelograms 1¼″ × 3⅝″.

VIOLET/GREEN LEAVES

1. Cut 8 squares 4¼″ × 4¼″; cut in half diagonally.

2. Cut 8 squares 4″ × 4″; cut in half diagonally.

3. Cut 8 squares 2″ × 2″; cut in half diagonally.

MEDIUM GREEN

1. Cut 8 trapezoids 1⅝″ × 4¼″.

2. Cut 8 trapezoids 1⅝″ × 3⅛″.

MEDIUM VIOLET

Cut 24 squares 2″ × 2″; cut in half diagonally.

SMALL SIDE BLOCK A & B

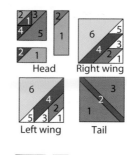

Head Right wing
Left wing Tail

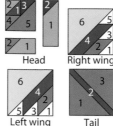

Head Right wing
Left wing Tail

Finished size: 6¾″ × 6¾″
Make 8 of each block.

LIGHT TURQUOISE FLORAL

Cut 16 squares 4¼″ × 4¼″; cut in half diagonally.

DARK BLUE

1. Cut 8 squares 2″ × 2″; cut in half diagonally.

2. Cut 32 parallelograms 1¼″ × 5¼″.

3. Cut 16 rectangles ⅞″ × 5½″.

VIOLET/GREEN LEAVES

Cut 16 squares 2″ × 2″; cut in half diagonally.

MEDIUM GREEN

1. Cut 16 trapezoids 1⅝″ × 4¼″.

2. Cut 16 trapezoids 1⅝″ × 3⅛″.

MEDIUM VIOLET

Cut 8 squares 2″ × 2″; cut in half diagonally.

WHITE

Cut 48 squares 2″ × 2″; cut in half diagonally.

VIOLET/GREEN FLORAL

1. Cut 8 squares 3⅛″ × 3⅛″; cut in half diagonally.

2. Cut 32 parallelograms 1¼″ × 3⅝″.

DARK VIOLET

Cut 16 squares 2″ × 2″; cut in half diagonally.

DARK GREEN

Cut 16 squares 4″ × 4″; cut in half diagonally.

SMALL CORNER BLOCK

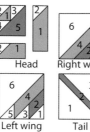

Head Right wing
Left wing Tail

Finished size: 6¾″ × 6¾″
Make 8 blocks.

MEDIUM VIOLET

1. Cut 4 squares 2″ × 2″; cut in half diagonally.

2. Cut 16 parallelograms 1¼″ × 5¼″.

3. Cut 8 trapezoids 1⅝″ × 4¼″.

4. Cut 8 trapezoids 1⅝″ × 3⅛″.

WHITE

1. Cut 44 squares 2″ × 2″; cut in half diagonally.

2. Cut 8 squares 4¼″ × 4¼″; cut in half diagonally.

3. Cut 8 squares 4″ × 4″; cut in half diagonally.

VIOLET/GREEN FLORAL

1. Cut 8 rectangles ⅞″ × 5½″.

2. Cut 4 squares 3⅛″ × 3⅛″; cut in half diagonally.

3. Cut 16 parallelograms 1¼″ × 3⅝″.

LARGE CENTER BLOCK CONSTRUCTION

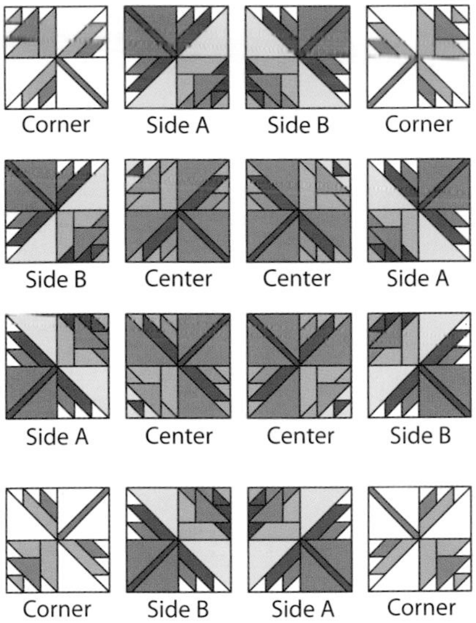
Corner
Side A
Side B
Corner
Side B
Center
Center
Side A
Side A
Center
Center
Side B
Corner
Side B
Side A
Corner

Finished size: 27″ × 27″
Make 2 blocks.

Press carefully as each piece is sewn.

1. For each large block, arrange and sew the small center, side, and corner blocks into 4 rows.

2. Sew the rows together to make 2 blocks.

LARGE SIDE BLOCK

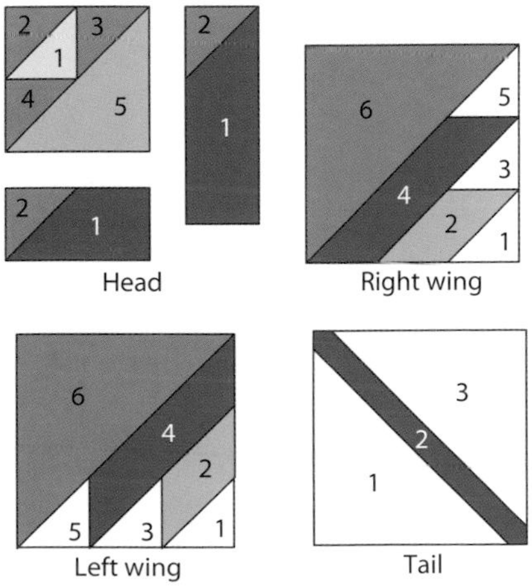
Head
Right wing
Left wing
Tail

Finished size: 13½″ × 13½″
Make 24 blocks.

LIGHT TURQUOISE FLORAL

Cut 12 squares 3⅛″ × 3⅛″; cut in half diagonally.

DARK BLUE

1. Cut 48 parallelograms 2⅛″ × 9¼″.

2. Cut 24 rectangles 1¼″ × 10¼″.

3. Cut 24 trapezoids 2¾″ × 7⅝″.

4. Cut 24 trapezoids 2¾″ × 5⅜″.

MEDIUM GREEN

1. Cut 12 squares 5⅜″ × 5⅜″; cut in half diagonally.

2. Cut 48 parallelograms 2⅛″ × 6″.

WHITE

1. Cut 24 squares 7″ × 7″; cut in half diagonally.

2. Cut 72 squares 3⅛″ × 3⅛″; cut in half diagonally.

VIOLET/GREEN FLORAL

1. Cut 24 squares 7⅝″ × 7⅝″; cut in half diagonally.

2. Cut 60 squares 3⅛″ × 3⅛″; cut in half diagonally.

> *Large Corner Block*
> Each large corner block is composed of 16 smaller 6¾″ square Dragonfly blocks.

SMALL CENTER BLOCK

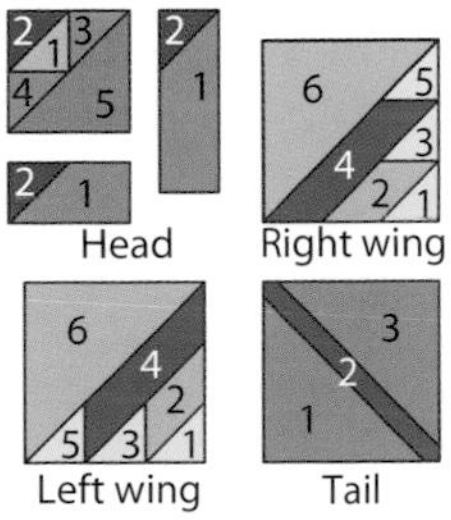
Head
Right wing
Left wing
Tail

Finished size: 6¾″ × 6¾″
Make 16 blocks.

LIGHT TURQUOISE FLORAL

Cut 48 squares 2″ × 2″; cut in half diagonally.

DARK BLUE

1. Cut 16 rectangles ⅞″ × 5½″.

2. Cut 32 parallelograms 1¼″ × 5¼″.

VIOLET/GREEN LEAVES

1. Cut 16 squares 2″ × 2″; cut in half diagonally.

2. Cut 16 trapezoids 1⅝″ × 4¼″.

3. Cut 16 trapezoids 1⅝″ × 3⅛″.

4. Cut 16 squares 4″ × 4″; cut in half diagonally.

MEDIUM GREEN

1. Cut 32 parallelograms 1¼″ × 3⅝″.

2. Cut 8 squares 4¼″ × 4¼″; cut in half diagonally.

3. Cut 8 squares 2″ × 2″; cut in half diagonally.

DARK VIOLET

Cut 24 squares 2″ × 2″; cut in half diagonally.

DARK GREEN

Cut 8 squares 3⅛″ × 3⅛″; cut in half diagonally.

SMALL SIDE BLOCK

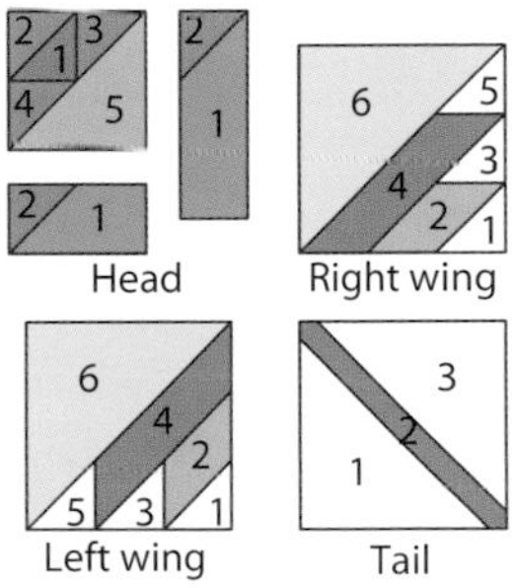
Head
Right wing
Left wing
Tail

Finished size: 6¾″ × 6¾″
Make 32 blocks.

LIGHT TURQUOISE FLORAL

Cut 32 squares 4¼″ × 4¼″; cut in half diagonally.

TURQUOISE

1. Cut 32 trapezoids 1⅝″ × 4¼″.

2. Cut 32 trapezoids 1⅝″ × 3⅛″.

VIOLET/GREEN LEAVES

Cut 80 squares 2″ × 2″; cut in half diagonally.

MEDIUM GREEN

1. Cut 64 parallelograms 1¼″ × 3⅝″.

2. Cut 16 squares 3⅛″ × 3⅛″; cut in half diagonally.

WHITE

1. Cut 96 squares 2″ × 2″; cut in half diagonally.

2. Cut 32 squares 4″ × 4″; cut in half diagonally.

DARK GREEN

1. Cut 32 rectangles ⅞″ × 5½″.

2. Cut 16 squares 2″ × 2″; cut in half diagonally.

3. Cut 64 parallelograms 1¼″ × 5¼″.

SMALL CORNER BLOCK A

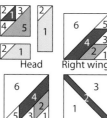

Finished size: 6¾″ × 6¾″
Make 12 blocks.

LIGHT TURQUOISE FLORAL

1. Cut 12 trapezoids 1⅝″ × 4¼″.

2. Cut 12 trapezoids 1⅝″ × 3⅛″.

DARK BLUE

1. Cut 6 squares 2″ × 2″; cut in half diagonally.

---

2. Cut 24 parallelograms 1¼″ × 5¼″.

3. Cut 12 rectangles ⅞″ × 5½″.

MEDIUM VIOLET

1. Cut 6 squares 3⅛″ × 3⅛″; cut in half diagonally.

2. Cut 24 parallelograms 1¼″ × 3⅝″.

WHITE

1. Cut 66 squares 2″ × 2″; cut in half diagonally.

2. Cut 12 squares 4¼″ × 4¼″; cut in half diagonally.

3. Cut 12 squares 4″ × 4″; cut in half diagonally.

SMALL CORNER BLOCK B

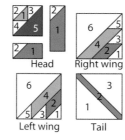

Finished size: 6¾″ × 6¾″
Make 4 blocks.

DARK BLUE

Cut 2 squares 3⅛″ × 3⅛″; cut in half diagonally.

MEDIUM VIOLET

1. Cut 2 squares 2″ × 2″; cut in half diagonally.

2. Cut 8 parallelograms 1¼″ × 5¼″.

WHITE

1. Cut 4 squares 4¼″ × 4¼″; cut in half diagonally.

---

2. Cut 4 squares 4″ × 4″; cut in half diagonally.

3. Cut 22 squares 2″ × 2″; cut in half diagonally.

VIOLET/GREEN FLORAL

1. Cut 8 parallelograms 1¼″ × 3⅝″.

2. Cut 4 trapezoids 1⅝″ × 4¼″.

3. Cut 4 trapezoids 1⅝″ × 3⅛″.

4. Cut 4 rectangles ⅞″ × 5½″.

LARGE CORNER BLOCK CONSTRUCTION

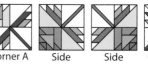

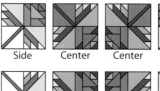

Finished size: 27″ × 27″
Make 4 blocks.

Press carefully as each piece is sewn.

1. For each large block, arrange and sew the small center, side, and corner blocks into 4 rows, placing the Corner B block toward the quilt center.

2. Join the rows.

Quilt Construction

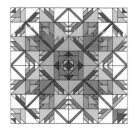

Corner

Side

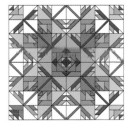

Corner

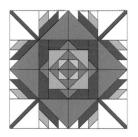

Side

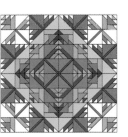

Center

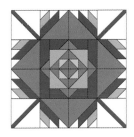

Side

Side

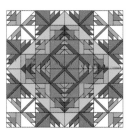

Center

Side

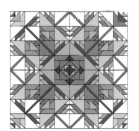

Corner

Side

Corner

Assembly diagram

1. Arrange and sew the large side blocks to make 6 blocks.

2. Arrange and sew the large center, side, and corner blocks into 4 rows.

3. Sew the rows together.

Quilting

Contour stitching emphasizes specific large motifs. Small decorative machine stitches are used to quilt the layers together while emphasizing specific pieces of the Dragonfly block. Stitch-in-the-ditch quilting is used in places that need some extra invisible quilting.

lilypad

Quilt size: 45˝ × 45˝
Finished block sizes: 9˝ × 9˝, 18˝ × 18˝

This quilt uses Dragonfly Block 1, which is changed to show a large inward-facing 18˝ Dragonfly block with smaller outward-facing 9˝ blocks replacing the larger motif's tail. Color placement creates the illusion of a large inner square, turned on point, with central Flying Geese. The head section of each block contains fussy-cut motifs to create a radiating pattern. If the motif in your print doesn't mirror itself, just rotate the squares as in *Sparkling Spring Afternoon* (page 50).

Make the blocks following the Dragonfly Block 1 piecing order on page 20.

Fussy-cut head square

Materials

■ Red/violet batik: 1⅝ yards (including borders)

■ Light blue: ⅜ yard

■ Light print with motif: ½ yard (40 motifs total)

■ Light gold: ¾ yard (including border)

■ Dark turquoise: ¼ yard

■ Dark green: ⅓ yard

■ Medium gold: ⅓ yard

■ Binding: ⅝ yard

■ Backing: 2¾ yards

■ Batting: 49˝ × 49˝

SMALL DRAGONFLY BLOCK

Head

Right wing

Left wing

Tail

Finished size: 9˝ × 9˝
Make 4 blocks.

RED/VIOLET BATIK

1. Cut 22 squares 2⅜˝ × 2⅜˝; cut in half diagonally.

2. Cut 4 squares 5″ × 5″; cut in half diagonally.

3. Cut 4 squares 5⅜″ × 5⅜″; cut in half diagonally.

LIGHT BLUE

1. Cut 18 squares 2⅜″ × 2⅜″; cut in half diagonally.

2. Cut 4 rectangles 1″ × 7⅛″.

LIGHT PRINT

Cut 16 squares 2″ × 2″, each with the same isolated motif.

LIGHT GOLD

Cut 4 squares 3⅞″ × 3⅞″; cut in half diagonally.

LARGE DRAGONFLY BLOCK

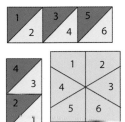
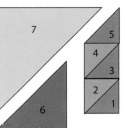

Head

Right wing

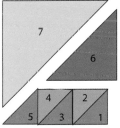
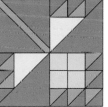

Left wing

Small dragonfly block

Finished size: 18″ × 10″
Make 4 blocks.

RED/VIOLET BATIK

Cut 12 squares 3⅞″ × 3⅞″; cut in half diagonally.

LIGHT BLUE

Cut 8 squares 3⅞″ × 3⅞″; cut in half diagonally.

LIGHT PRINT

Cut 24 triangles approximately 4″ high with a 60° angle. Each triangle should have the same isolated motif. For each block, sew 6 triangles together, center on a cutting mat, and cut a 6½″ square.

LIGHT GOLD

Cut 10 squares 3⅞″ × 3⅞″; cut in half diagonally.

DARK TURQUOISE

Cut 10 squares 3⅞″ × 3⅞″; cut in half diagonally.

DARK GREEN

Cut 4 squares 6⅞″ × 6⅞″; cut in half diagonally.

MEDIUM GOLD

Cut 4 squares 9⅞″ × 9⅞″; cut in half diagonally.

Quilt Construction

Press carefully as each piece is sewn.

1. Sew the 4 small blocks, then sew the 4 large blocks together.

2. Cut 2 border strips 2″ × 36½″ from red/violet batik. Sew to the sides of the quilt.

3. Cut 2 border strips 2″ × 39½″ from red/violet batik. Sew to the top and bottom of the quilt.

4. Cut 2 border strips 2″ × 39½″ from light gold. Sew to the sides of the quilt.

5. Make 2 border strips 2″ × 42½″ of light gold. Sew to the top and bottom of the quilt.

6. Make 2 border strips 2″ × 42½″ of red/violet batik. Sew to the sides of the quilt.

7. Make 2 border strips 2″ × 45½″ of red/violet batik. Sew to the top and bottom of the quilt.

Quilting

Decorative stitching is a large part of this quilt. A circle motif, placed in the plain triangles of the inner square, is outlined with a dark, variegated thread using a decorative stitch. Heavy background stitching in small circles further emphasizes the circle motif. Half circles in the inner green triangles and around the inner border band complete the quilt.

Stitched motifs

oasis

Quilt size: 72˝ × 90˝
Finished block size: 18˝ × 18˝

Because the trapezoids are mirror images in the block, cut half of the pieces angled right and half angled left. Make the center blocks following the Dragonfly Block 5 piecing order for the wings on page 22. Make the side and corner blocks following the Dragonfly Block 4 piecing order on page 21.

Materials

- Light gold: 1 yard
- Blue batik: ⅜ yard
- Green batik: ¾ yard
- Light beige: 1½ yards
- Brown: ¾ yard
- Light green: 2¾ yards of one fabric or 3¼ yards total of assorted fabrics for pieced background
- Turquoise: 1¼ yards
- Dark gold: 1¼ yards
- Binding: ¾ yard
- Backing: 5⅓ yards
- Batting: 76˝ × 94˝

PIECED BACKGROUND

ASSORTED LIGHT GREENS

Cut 600 squares 2⅝˝ × 2⅝˝. Place on point, and sew together to create background pieces.

This quilt uses two Dragonfly blocks, the full Dragonfly Block 4, and the double wings from Block 5. The center block has a double wing and three tails. Several light green fabrics make up the outermost large background portions of this quilt. These were cut into small (2⅛˝ finished size) squares, and then turned on point. This creates a visual density in the background that you don't see in the other quilts. If you would rather not piece the background, use a single light green fabric. The blocks are set on a vertically staggered grid.

CENTER BLOCK

 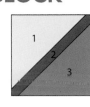

 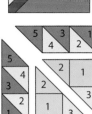 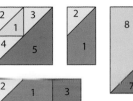

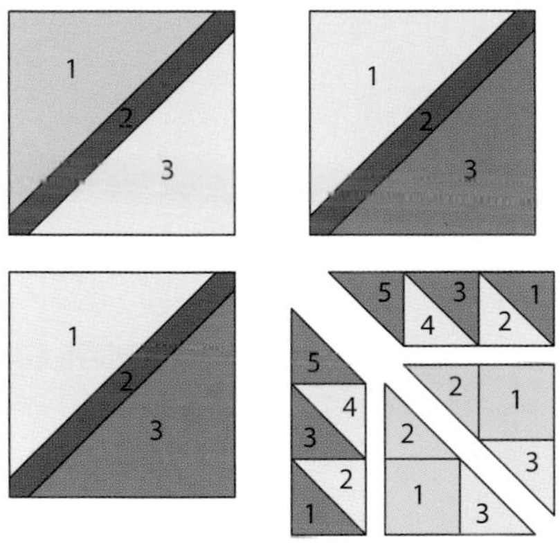

Finished size: 18˝ × 18˝
Make 4 blocks.

LIGHT GOLD

Cut 4 squares 3⅞˝ × 3⅞˝; cut in half diagonally.

BLUE BATIK

1. Cut 4 squares 3⅞˝ × 3⅞˝; cut in half diagonally.

2. Cut 8 squares 3½˝ × 3½˝.

GREEN BATIK

1. Cut 12 squares 3⅞˝ × 3⅞˝; cut in half diagonally.

2. Cut 4 squares 9⅛˝ × 9⅛˝; cut in half diagonally.

LIGHT BEIGE

1. Cut 8 squares 3⅞˝ × 3⅞˝; cut in half diagonally.

2. Cut 6 squares 9⅛˝ × 9⅛˝; cut in half diagonally.

BROWN

Cut 12 rectangles 1½˝ × 13½˝.

LIGHT GREEN

Cut 2 squares 9⅛˝ × 9⅛˝; cut in half diagonally.

SIDE BLOCK A & B

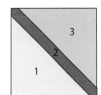

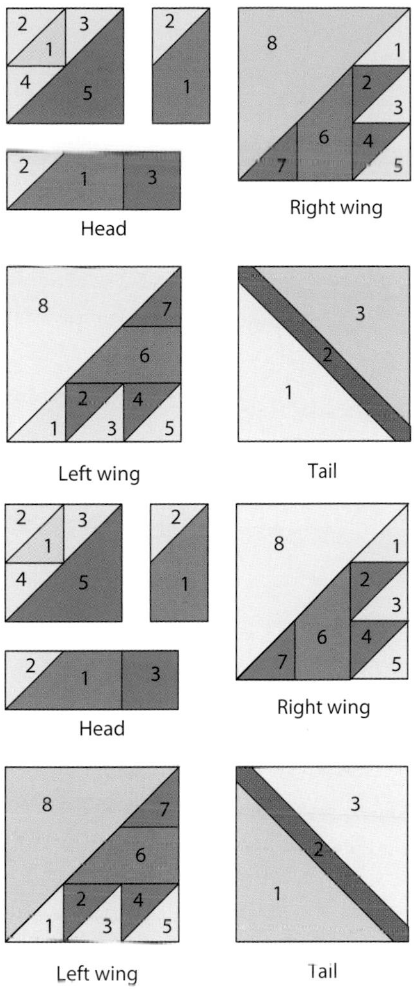

Head   Right wing

Left wing   Tail

Head   Right wing

Left wing   Tail

Finished size: 18˝ × 18˝
Make 4 of each block.

LIGHT GOLD

Cut 44 squares 3⅞˝ × 3⅞˝; cut in half diagonally.

BLUE BATIK

Cut 4 squares 3⅞˝ × 3⅞˝; cut in half diagonally.

LIGHT BEIGE

1. Cut 4 squares 9⅛˝ × 9⅛˝; cut in half diagonally.

2. Cut 4 squares 9⅞˝ × 9⅞˝; cut in half diagonally.

BROWN

Cut 8 rectangles 1½˝ × 13½˝.

LIGHT GREEN

1. Cut 4 squares 9⅛˝ × 9⅛˝; cut in half diagonally.

2. Cut 4 squares 9⅞˝ × 9⅞˝; cut in half diagonally.

TURQUOISE

1. Cut 24 squares 3⅞˝ × 3⅞˝; cut in half diagonally.

2. Cut 4 squares 6⅞˝ × 6⅞˝; cut in half diagonally.

3. Cut 8 squares 3½˝ × 3½˝.

DARK GOLD

Cut 32 trapezoids 3½˝ × 6⅞˝.

CORNER BLOCK

 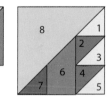

Head   Right wing

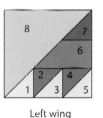 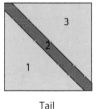

Left wing   Tail

Finished size: 18˝ × 18˝
Make 4 blocks.

LIGHT GOLD

Cut 22 squares 3⅞˝ × 3⅞˝; cut in half diagonally.

BLUE BATIK

Cut 2 squares 3⅞˝ × 3⅞˝; cut in half diagonally.

BROWN

1. Cut 4 rectangles 1½˝ × 13½˝.

2. Cut 4 squares 3⅞˝ × 3⅞˝; cut in half diagonally.

LIGHT GREEN

1. Cut 4 squares 9⅞" × 9⅞"; cut in half diagonally.

2. Cut 4 squares 9⅛" × 9⅛"; cut in half diagonally.

TURQUOISE

1. Cut 4 squares 3½" × 3½".

2. Cut 2 squares 6⅞" × 6⅞"; cut in half diagonally.

3. Cut 8 squares 3⅞" × 3⅞"; cut in half diagonally.

DARK GOLD

Cut 16 trapezoids 3½" × 6⅞".

Press carefully as each piece is sewn.

1. Cut 16 squares 9½" × 9½" of light green.

2. Sew the light green squares into pairs, forming rectangles.

3. Sew the rectangles to the top or bottom of the corner blocks and 4 of the side blocks, as shown in the diagram.

4. Arrange and sew into 2 rows.

5. Arrange and sew the center and remaining side blocks into 2 rows.

6. Arrange and sew the rows together.

Quilt Construction

Corner

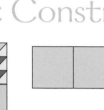

Side A

Side B

Corner

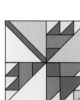

Side A

Side B

Side B

Center

Center

Side A

Side A

Center

Center

Side B

Side A

Center

Center

Side B

Side B

Side A

Corner

Corner

Assembly diagram

Quilting

Because this is such a visually dense quilt, the quilting stitches have been kept simple. There is a mix of decorative stitches, mainly in the tail sections. Wandering vine and stippling stitches are used in the quilt body.

Detail of quilting

Quilt size: 60˝ × 60˝
Finished block sizes: 9 × 9˝, 18˝ × 18˝

Materials

- Blue snail print: ⅔ yard
- Medium green: ⅓ yard
- Creamy white: 1⅜ yards
- Dark red/violet: ⅔ yard
- Light beige: ¼ yard
- Blue leaf: 1⅛ yards
- Gold batik: 1¾ yards (including borders)
- Dark green: ⅓ yard
- Binding: ⅝ yard
- Backing: 3⅔ yards
- Batting: 64˝ × 64˝

DOUBLE SQUARE

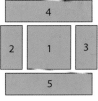

Finished size: 3˝ × 3˝
Make 40 double squares.

BLUE SNAIL PRINT

1. Cut 80 rectangles 1¼˝ × 2˝.

2. Cut 80 rectangles 1¼˝ × 3½˝.

MEDIUM GREEN

Cut 40 squares 2˝ × 2˝.

This quilt is a nine patch that uses Dragonfly Block 2. The center block is a double wing block that has been modified so that there is a diamond within a square in the center. This adds visual interest, echoing the surrounding diamond-within-square motifs. A large star is formed by using a bright fabric in the plain wing sections. Finally, changing the small squares in the Dragonfly block creates a smaller square within the larger square.

Because both the parallelograms and trapezoids are mirror images in the block,

cut half of the pieces for each shape angled right and half angled left. Make the blocks following the Dragonfly Block 2 piecing order on page 20.

DOUBLE SQUARE CONSTRUCTION

1. Sew a 1¼″ × 2″ rectangle to either side of each 2″ square. Press.

2. Sew a 1¼″ × 3½″ rectangle to the top and bottom of each pieced square. Press.

CENTER BLOCK

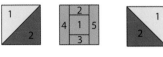

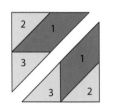

Finished size: 9″ × 9″
Make 4 blocks.

Use 8 Double Square blocks, 2 for each block.

CREAMY WHITE

Cut 6 squares 3⅞″ × 3⅞″; cut in half diagonally.

DARK RED/VIOLET

Cut 6 squares 3⅞″ × 3⅞″; cut in half diagonally.

LIGHT BEIGE

Cut 8 squares 3⅞″ × 3⅞″; cut in half diagonally.

BLUE LEAF

Cut 8 parallelograms 2⅝″ × 7⅞″.

SIDE BLOCK A & B

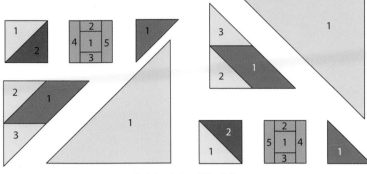

Finished size: 9″ × 9″
Make 8 of each block.

Use 16 Double Square blocks, 1 for each block.

CREAMY WHITE

Cut 24 squares 3⅞″ × 3⅞″; cut in half diagonally.

DARK RED/VIOLET

Cut 8 squares 3⅞″ × 3⅞″; cut in half diagonally.

BLUE LEAF

1. Cut 8 squares 3⅞″ × 3⅞″; cut in half diagonally.

2. Cut 16 parallelograms 2⅝″ × 7⅞″.

GOLD BATIK

Cut 8 squares 9⅞″ × 9⅞″; cut in half diagonally.

CORNER BLOCK

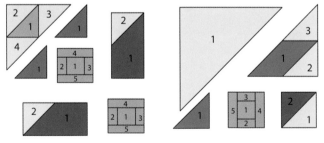

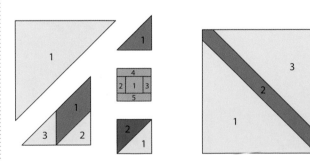

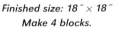

Finished size: 18″ × 18″
Make 4 blocks.

Use 16 Double Square blocks, 4 for each block.

MEDIUM GREEN

Cut 2 squares 3⅞″ × 3⅞″; cut in half diagonally.

CREAMY WHITE

1. Cut 22 squares 3⅞″ × 3⅞″; cut in half diagonally.

2. Cut 4 squares 9⅞″ × 9⅞″; cut in half diagonally.

3. Cut 4 squares 9⅛″ × 9⅛″; cut in half diagonally.

DARK RED/VIOLET

1. Cut 4 squares 3⅞″ × 3⅞″; cut in half diagonally.

2. Cut 8 trapezoids 3½″ × 6⅞″.

BLUE LEAF

1. Cut 4 squares 3⅞″ × 3⅞″; cut in half diagonally.

2. Cut 8 parallelograms 2⅝″ × 7⅝″.

DARK GREEN

1. Cut 4 squares 3⅞″ × 3⅞″; cut in half diagonally.

2. Cut 4 rectangles 1½″ × 13½″.

Quilt Construction

Corner

Side

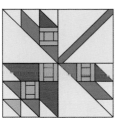
Corner

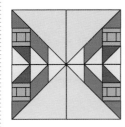
Side

Center

Side

Corner

Side

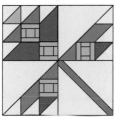
Corner

Assembly diagram

Press carefully as each piece is sewn.

1. Sew the 4 center blocks together.

2. Arrange and sew 2 each of side block A and B to make the side blocks.

3. Arrange and sew the center, side, and corner blocks into 3 rows.

4. Sew the rows together.

5. Make 2 border strips 3½″ × 54½″ of gold batik. Sew to the top and bottom of the quilt.

6. Make 2 border strips 3½″ × 60½″ of gold batik. Sew to the sides of the quilt.

Quilting

Simple decorative stitches have been used to create quilted motifs. They emphasize quilted motifs placed in the blank wing and tail areas.

spring fling

Quilt size: 75˝ × 75˝
Finished block size: 12˝ × 12˝

Materials

- Light gold: ¾ yard
- Dark brown: 1⅛ yards
- Light blue: ⅜ yard
- Medium blue: 1½ yards
- Dark gold: 2½ yards
- Light blue/green: ½ yard
- Medium green: ⅝ yard
- Dark green: 1¼ yards
- Medium gold: 1¼ yards
- Light brown: ¼ yard
- Light green: ½ yard
- Binding: ¾ yard
- Deep green for sashing: ⅔ yard
- Backing: 4½ yards
- Batting: 79˝ × 79˝

This quilt uses Dragonfly Block 4. It has many different textures created by using cotton, velveteen, and silk fabrics. A wandering vine quilting stitch and beading complete the quilt and add to the textural feel. There are 36 blocks in the quilt, 4 containing a small half-size block in place of the tail. The appearance of larger secondary motifs is created by color placement, and by the sashing strips, which give the impression of a border.

Because the trapezoids are mirror images in the block, cut half of the pieces angled right and half angled left. Make the blocks following the Dragonfly Block 4 piecing order on page 21.

CENTER BLOCK

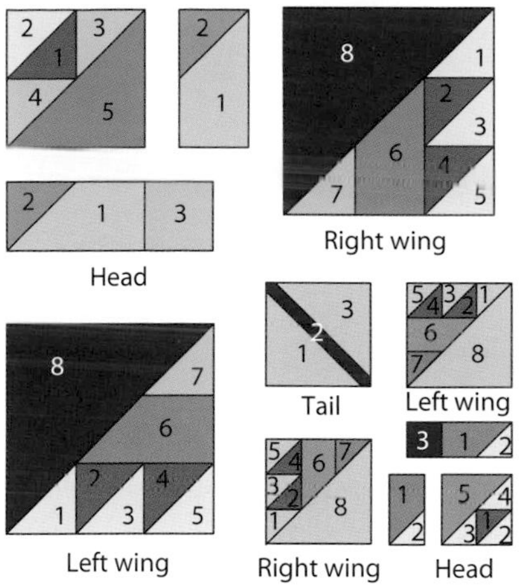
Right wing
Head
Tail
Left wing
Left wing
Right wing
Head

Finished size: 12″ × 12″
Make 4 blocks.

The center block has a head and two wing sections. The tail section is replaced by a half-sized full Dragonfly block.

LIGHT GOLD

1. Cut 14 squares 2⅞″ × 2⅞″; cut in half diagonally.
2. Cut 10 squares 1⅞″ × 1⅞″; cut in half diagonally.

DARK BROWN

1. Cut 10 squares 2⅞″ × 2⅞″; cut in half diagonally.
2. Cut 10 squares 1⅞″ × 1⅞″; cut in half diagonally.

LIGHT BLUE

Cut 4 squares 2⅞″ × 2⅞″; cut in half diagonally.

MEDIUM BLUE

1. Cut 8 trapezoids 2½″ × 4⅞″.
2. Cut 8 trapezoids 1½″ × 2⅞″.
3. Cut 2 squares 4⅞″ × 4⅞″; cut in half diagonally.
4. Cut 4 squares 1⅞″ × 1⅞″; cut in half diagonally.

DARK GOLD

1. Cut 8 trapezoids 2½″ × 4⅞″.
2. Cut 4 squares 3⅞″ × 3⅞″; cut in half diagonally.
3. Cut 4 squares 3⅝″ × 3⅝″; cut in half diagonally.
4. Cut 12 squares 1⅞″ × 1⅞″; cut in half diagonally.

LIGHT BLUE/GREEN

1. Cut 8 squares 2⅞″ × 2⅞″; cut in half diagonally.
2. Cut 4 squares 2½″ × 2½″.

MEDIUM GREEN

1. Cut 6 squares 2⅞″ × 2⅞″; cut in half diagonally.
2. Cut 8 trapezoids 1½″ × 2⅞″.

DARK GREEN

1. Cut 4 squares 6⅞″ × 6⅞″; cut in half diagonally.
2. Cut 4 squares 1½″ × 1½″.
3. Cut 4 rectangles ⅞″ × 5″.

SIDE BLOCK A & B

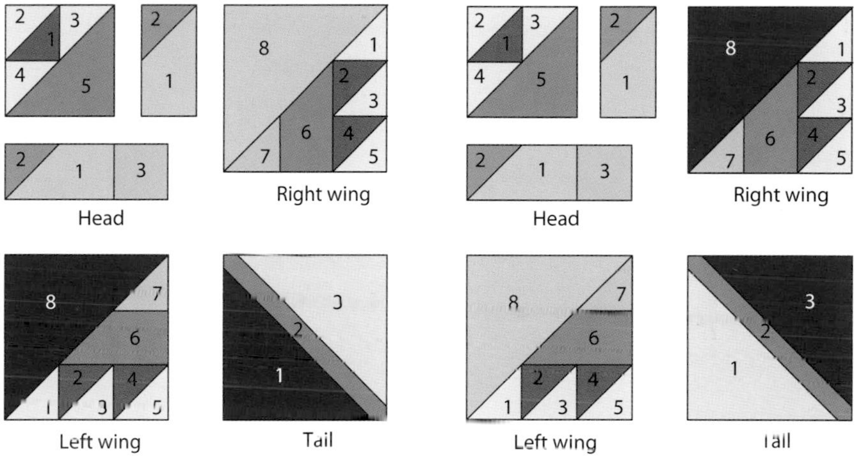
Head
Right wing
Head
Right wing
Left wing
Tail
Left wing
Tail

Finished size: 12″ × 12″
Make 4 of each block.

LIGHT GOLD

Cut 36 squares 2⅞″ × 2⅞″; cut in half diagonally.

DARK BROWN

Cut 20 squares 2⅞″ × 2⅞″; cut in half diagonally.

MEDIUM BLUE

1. Cut 16 trapezoids 2½″ × 4⅞″.
2. Cut 4 squares 4⅞″ × 4⅞″; cut in half diagonally.
3. Cut 8 rectangles 1¼″ × 9¼″.

DARK GOLD

1. Cut 16 trapezoids 2½″ × 4⅞″.
2. Cut 4 squares 6⅞″ × 6⅞″; cut in half diagonally.

LIGHT BLUE/GREEN

1. Cut 8 squares 2⅞″ × 2⅞″; cut in half diagonally.
2. Cut 8 squares 2½″ × 2½″.

MEDIUM GREEN

Cut 8 squares 2⅞″ × 2⅞″; cut in half diagonally.

DARK GREEN

1. Cut 4 squares 6⅜″ × 6⅜″; cut in half diagonally.
2. Cut 4 squares 6⅞″ × 6⅞″; cut in half diagonally.

MEDIUM GOLD

Cut 4 squares 6⅜″ × 6⅜″; cut in half diagonally.

CORNER BLOCK

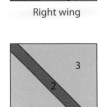

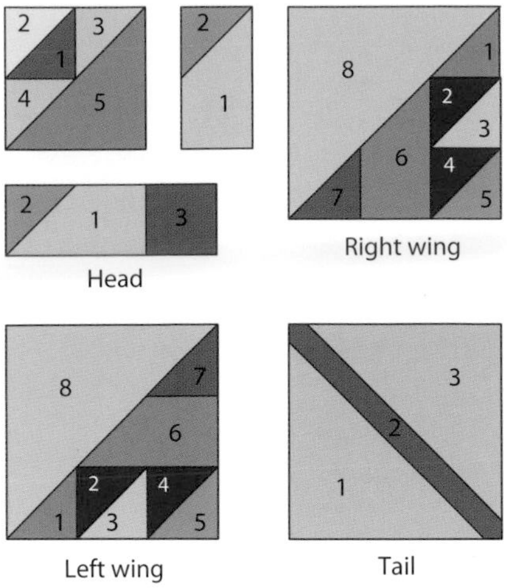

Head

Right wing

Left wing

Tail

Finished size: 12″ × 12″
Make 4 blocks.

LIGHT GOLD

Cut 2 squares 2⅞″ × 2⅞″; cut in half diagonally.

DARK BROWN

1. Cut 6 squares 2⅞″ × 2⅞″; cut in half diagonally.

2. Cut 4 squares 2½″ × 2½″.

3. Cut 4 rectangles 1¼″ × 9¼″.

LIGHT BLUE

Cut 8 squares 2⅞″ × 2⅞″; cut in half diagonally.

MEDIUM BLUE

1. Cut 8 trapezoids 2½″ × 4⅞″.

2. Cut 2 squares 4⅞″ × 4⅞″; cut in half diagonally.

DARK GOLD

1. Cut 8 trapezoids 2½″ × 4⅞″.

2. Cut 8 squares 6⅞″ × 6⅞″; cut in half diagonally.

MEDIUM GREEN

Cut 8 squares 2⅞″ × 2⅞″; cut in half diagonally.

DARK GREEN

Cut 8 squares 2⅞″ × 2⅞″; cut in half diagonally.

LIGHT BROWN

Cut 4 squares 2⅞″ × 2⅞″; cut in half diagonally.

LIGHT GREEN

Cut 4 squares 6⅜″ × 6⅜″; cut in half diagonally.

BORDER BLOCK A & B

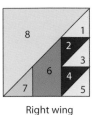

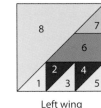

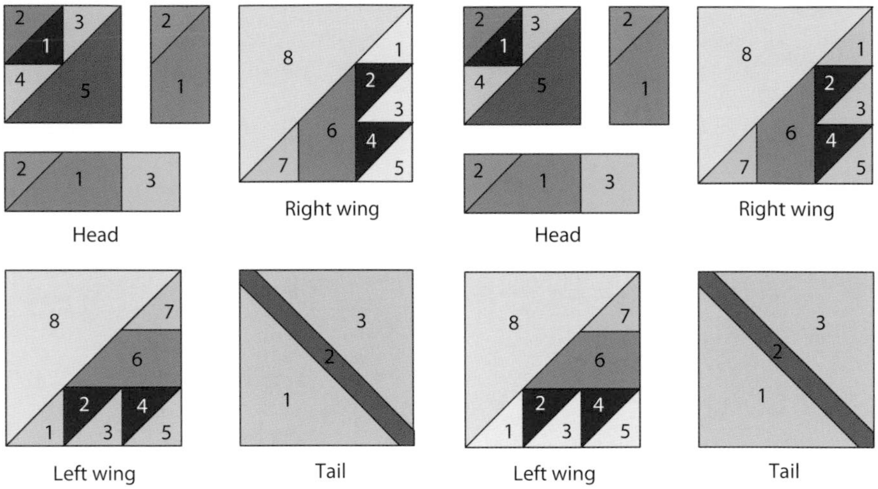

Head

Right wing

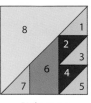

Head

Right wing

Left wing

Tail

Left wing

Tail

Finished size: 12″ × 12″
Make 4 of each block.

LIGHT GOLD

Cut 12 squares 2⅞″ × 2⅞″; cut in half diagonally.

DARK BROWN

1. Cut 4 squares 4⅞″ × 4⅞″; cut in half diagonally.

2. Cut 8 rectangles 1¼″ × 9¼″.

LIGHT BLUE

Cut 8 squares 2⅞″ × 2⅞″; cut in half diagonally.

MEDIUM BLUE

Cut 32 trapezoids 2½″ × 4⅞″.

DARK GOLD

1. Cut 12 squares 2⅞″ × 2⅞″; cut in half diagonally.

2. Cut 8 squares 6⅜″ × 6⅜″; cut in half diagonally.

LIGHT BLUE/GREEN

1. Cut 8 squares 2⅞″ × 2⅞″; cut in half diagonally.

2. Cut 8 squares 2½″ × 2½″.

MEDIUM GREEN

Cut 8 squares 2⅞″ × 2⅞″; cut in half diagonally.

DARK GREEN

Cut 20 squares 2⅞″ × 2⅞″; cut in half diagonally.

MEDIUM GOLD

Cut 8 squares 6⅞″ × 6⅞″; cut in half diagonally.

LIGHT BROWN

Cut 4 squares 2⅞″ × 2⅞″; cut in half diagonally.

BORDER BLOCK C

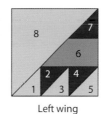

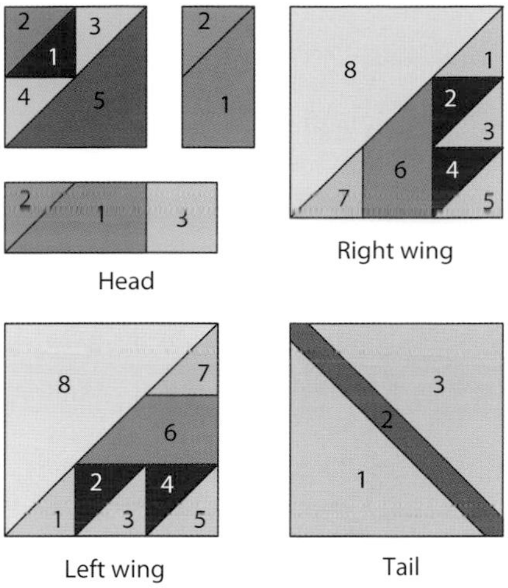

Head

Right wing

Left wing

Tail

Finished size: 12˝ × 12˝
Make 8 blocks.

DARK BROWN

1. Cut 8 rectangles 1¼˝ × 9¼˝.

2. Cut 4 squares 4⅞˝ × 4⅞˝; cut in half diagonally.

LIGHT BLUE

Cut 8 squares 2⅞˝ × 2⅞˝; cut in half diagonally.

MEDIUM BLUE

Cut 32 trapezoids 2½˝ × 4⅞˝.

DARK GOLD

1. Cut 24 squares 2⅞˝ × 2⅞˝; cut in half diagonally.

2. Cut 8 squares 6⅜˝ × 6⅜˝; cut in half diagonally.

LIGHT BLUE/GREEN

Cut 8 squares 2½˝ × 2½˝.

MEDIUM GREEN

Cut 8 squares 2⅞˝ × 2⅞˝; cut in half diagonally.

DARK GREEN

Cut 20 squares 2⅞˝ × 2⅞˝; cut in half diagonally.

MEDIUM GOLD

Cut 8 squares 6⅞˝ × 6⅞˝; cut in half diagonally.

LIGHT BROWN

Cut 4 squares 2⅞˝ × 2⅞˝; cut in half diagonally.

LIGHT GREEN

Cut 8 squares 2⅞˝ × 2⅞˝; cut in half diagonally.

BORDER CORNER

Head

Right wing

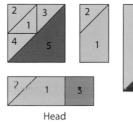

Left wing

Tail

Finished size: 12˝ × 12˝
Make 4 blocks.

DARK BROWN

Cut 2 squares 4⅞˝ × 4⅞˝; cut in half diagonally.

LIGHT BLUE

Cut 2 squares 2⅞˝ × 2⅞˝; cut in half diagonally.

MEDIUM BLUE

1. Cut 8 trapezoids 2½˝ × 4⅞˝.

2. Cut 4 squares 2½˝ × 2½˝.

3. Cut 4 rectangles 1¼˝ × 9¼˝.

DARK GOLD

1. Cut 4 squares 6⅜˝ × 6⅜˝; cut in half diagonally.

2. Cut 4 squares 6⅞˝ × 6⅞˝; cut in half diagonally.

3. Cut 22 squares 2⅞˝ × 2⅞˝; cut in half diagonally.

DARK GREEN

Cut 12 squares 2⅞˝ × 2⅞˝; cut in half diagonally.

LIGHT GREEN

Cut 8 trapezoids 2½˝ × 4⅞˝.

Quilt Construction

| Border Corner | Border C | Border A | Border B | Border C | Border Corner |

| Border C | Corner | Side A | Side B | Corner | Border C |

| Border B | Side B | Center | Center | Side A | Border A |

| Border A | Side A | Center | Center | Side B | Border B |

| Border C | Corner | Side B | Side A | Corner | Border C |

| Border Corner | Border C | Border B | Border A | Border C | Border Corner |

Assembly diagram

Press carefully as each piece is sewn.

1. Arrange and sew the center, side, and corner blocks into 4 rows.

2. Sew the rows together to make the center section of the quilt.

3. Make 2 border strips 2"x 48½" of deep green. Sew to the top and bottom of the center section.

4. Arrange and sew border blocks A, B, and C to make the top and bottom borders. Sew to the center section.

5. Make 2 border strips 2"x 75½" of deep green. Sew to the sides of the center section.

6. Cut 4 strips 2"x 12½" of deep green. Arrange and sew the remaining border blocks and the strips to make the side borders. Sew to the sides of the center section.

Quilting

A wandering vine motif has been used to stitch the entire quilt. This adds a subtle texture to the quilt. Beading emphasizes the vine motif while adding sparkle to the quilt.

dragonfly moon

Quilt size: 72″ × 72″
Finished block sizes: 10½″ × 10½″, 15″ × 15″

This quilt uses Dragonfly Block 6. Four small outwardly radiating Dragonfly blocks are turned on point in the center of this quilt. The center becomes part of a square created by adding plain triangles and Dragonfly head blocks. The corner blocks are outwardly radiating Dragonfly blocks. The quilt design is completed by double wing and tail blocks.

Because the parallelograms are mirror images in the block, cut half of the pieces angled right and half angled left. Make the blocks following the Dragonfly Block 6 piecing order on page 22.

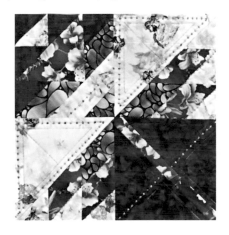

Materials

■ Dark blue: 4 yards (including borders)

■ Light blue: 2 yards

■ Violet/green floral: 1 yard

■ Blue floral: 2 yards (including borders)

■ Medium blue: ⅔ yard

■ Binding: ⅔ yard

■ Backing: 4⅓ yards

■ Batting: 76″ × 76″

SMALL CENTER BLOCK

Head

Right wing

Left wing

Tail

Finished size: 10½″ × 10½″
Make 4 blocks.

DARK BLUE

1. Cut 4 squares 5¾″ × 5¾″; cut in half diagonally.

2. Cut 4 squares 6⅛″ × 6⅛″; cut in half diagonally.

3. Cut 22 squares 2⅝″ × 2⅝″; cut in half diagonally.

LIGHT BLUE

1. Cut 4 squares 2⅝″ × 2⅝″; cut in half diagonally.

2. Cut 16 parallelograms 1¾″ × 5″.

VIOLET/GREEN FLORAL

1. Cut 2 squares 4⅜″ × 4⅜″; cut in half diagonally.

2. Cut 8 parallelograms 1¾″ × 5″.

BLUE FLORAL

1. Cut 8 parallelograms 1¾″ × 5″.

2. Cut 4 quadrilaterals 1¾″ × 6¼″.

3. Cut 4 rectangles 1⅛″ × 8⅛″.

CENTER TRIANGLE BLOCK

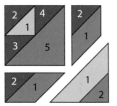
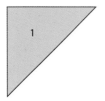

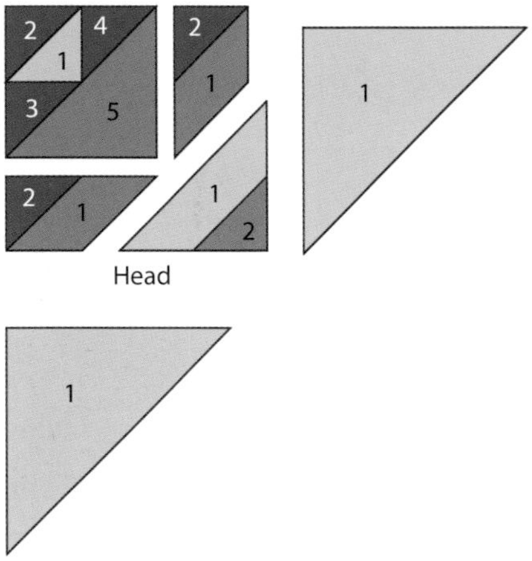

Head

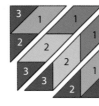

Finished size: 7½″ block,
15″ completed triangle
Make 4 blocks.

DARK BLUE

Cut 10 squares 3⅜″ × 3⅜″; cut in half diagonally.

LIGHT BLUE

1. Cut 4 squares 8⅜″ × 8⅜″; cut in half diagonally.

2. Cut 2 squares 3⅜″ × 3⅜″; cut in half diagonally.

3. Cut 4 quadrilaterals 2¼″ × 8⅜″.

VIOLET/GREEN FLORAL

1. Cut 2 squares 3⅜″ × 3⅜″; cut in half diagonally.

2. Cut 8 parallelograms 2¼″ × 6½″.

BLUE FLORAL

Cut 2 squares 5⅞″ × 5⅞″; cut in half diagonally.

SIDE BLOCK

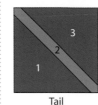

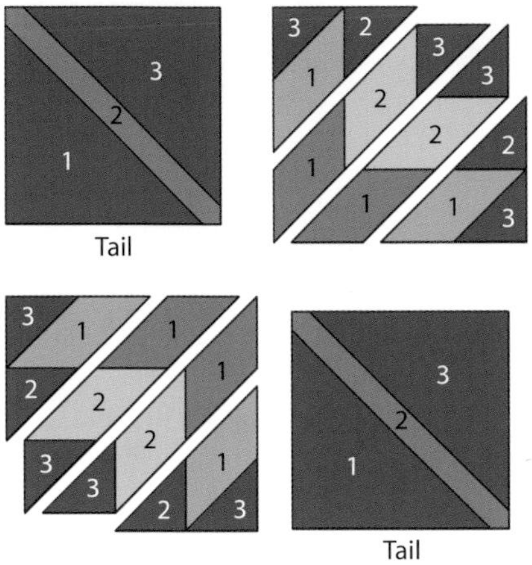

Tail

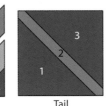

Tail

Finished size: 15″ × 15″
Make 8 blocks.

DARK BLUE

1. Cut 16 squares 7¾″ × 7¾″; cut in half diagonally.

2. Cut 48 squares 3⅜″ × 3⅜″; cut in half diagonally.

LIGHT BLUE

Cut 32 parallelograms 2¼″ × 6½″.

BLUE FLORAL

1. Cut 16 rectangles 1⅜″ × 11⅜″.

2. Cut 32 parallelograms 2¼″ × 6½″.

MEDIUM BLUE

Cut 32 parallelograms 2¼″ × 6½″.

CORNER BLOCK

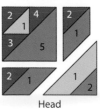
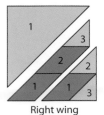

Head   Right wing

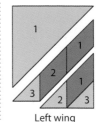
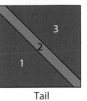

Left wing   Tail

Finished size: 15″ × 15″
Make 4 blocks.

DARK BLUE

1. Cut 4 squares 7¾″ × 7¾″; cut in half diagonally.

2. Cut 10 squares 3⅜″ × 3⅜″; cut in half diagonally.

LIGHT BLUE

1. Cut 14 squares 3⅜″ × 3⅜″; cut in half diagonally.

2. Cut 4 quadrilaterals 2¼″ × 8⅜″.

3. Cut 4 squares 8⅜″ × 8⅜″; cut in half diagonally.

VIOLET/GREEN FLORAL

1. Cut 16 parallelograms 2¼″ × 6½″.

2. Cut 2 squares 3⅜″ × 3⅜″; cut in half diagonally.

BLUE FLORAL

1. Cut 16 parallelograms 2¼″ × 6½″.

2. Cut 2 squares 5⅞″ × 5⅞″; cut in half diagonally.

3. Cut 4 rectangles 1⅜″ × 11⅜″.

Quilt Construction

Corner

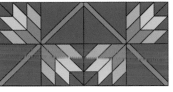

Side

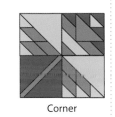

Corner

Side

Center

Side

Side

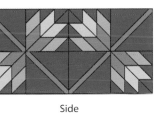

Corner

Side

Corner

Assembly diagram

Press carefully as each piece is sewn.

1. Sew the 4 small center blocks together.

2. Sew the center triangles to each side of the center blocks.

3. Sew the side blocks together in pairs.

4. Arrange and sew the center section, side block sections, and corner blocks into 3 rows.

5. Sew the rows together.

6. Make 2 border strips 3″ × 60½″ of dark blue. Sew to the sides of the quilt.

7. Make 2 border strips 3″ × 65½″ of dark blue. Sew to the top and bottom of the quilt.

8. Make 2 border strips 1½″ × 65½″ of blue floral. Sew to the sides of the quilt.

9. Make 2 border strips 1½″ × 67½″ of blue floral. Sew to the top and bottom of the quilt.

10. Make 2 border strips 3″ × 67½″ of dark blue. Sew to the sides of the quilt.

11. Make 2 border strips 3″ × 72½″ of dark blue. Sew to the top and bottom of the quilt.

Quilting

A simple ball-and-line decorative stitch has been used to emphasize some larger light motifs. A stitched grid pattern further emphasizes some of these motifs. The remainder of the quilt has been stitched with fine parallel lines. A decorative large zigzag accents the inner border.

desert dragonfly

Quilt size: 38˝ × 38˝
Finished block sizes: 9˝ × 9˝, 4½˝ × 18˝, 4½˝ x 4½˝, 6⅜˝ × 6⅜˝

Materials

- Off white: 1¼ yards (including borders)
- Green: ¾ yard
- Dark rust/turquoise batik: ½ yard
- Dark turquoise: ⅝ yard
- Dark blue: ½ yard
- Light rust: ½ yard
- Binding: ½ yard
- Backing: 1¼ yards
- Batting: 42˝ × 42˝

CENTER BLOCK

Head — Right wing

Left wing — Tail

Finished size: 9˝ × 9˝
Make 4 blocks.

OFF-WHITE

Cut 22 squares 2⅜˝ × 2⅜˝; cut in half diagonally.

This quilt uses Dragonfly Block 2 and only six fabrics. It combines full Dragonfly blocks with Dragonfly head and wing blocks. Additionally, the center blocks are turned on point, while the remaining blocks are oriented conventionally. The result is a multitude of secondary designs, which have been emphasized by color use.

Because both the parallelograms and trapezoids are mirror images in the block, cut half of each shape angled right and half angled left. Make the blocks following the Dragonfly Block 2 piecing order on page 20.

GREEN

1. Cut 8 squares 2" × 2".

2. Cut 6 squares 2⅜" × 2⅜"; cut in half diagonally.

DARK RUST/TURQUOISE

1. Cut 4 squares 2" × 2".

2. Cut 8 parallelograms 1½" × 4½".

DARK TURQUOISE

1. Cut 4 squares 2⅜" × 2⅜"; cut in half diagonally.

2. Cut 8 trapezoids 2" × 3⅞".

DARK BLUE

1. Cut 4 squares 2" × 2".

2. Cut 4 squares 2⅜" × 2⅜"; cut in half diagonally.

3. Cut 4 rectangles 1" × 7⅛".

LIGHT RUST

1. Cut 4 squares 5⅜" × 5⅜"; cut in half diagonally.

2. Cut 4 squares 5" × 5"; cut in half diagonally.

SIDE BLOCK RECTANGLE

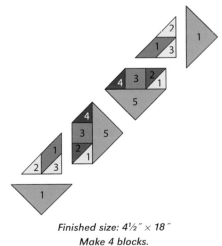

Finished size: 4½" × 18"
Make 4 blocks.

OFF-WHITE

Cut 12 squares 3" × 3"; cut in half diagonally.

GREEN

Cut 8 squares 2⅝" × 2⅝".

DARK RUST/TURQUOISE

Cut 8 parallelograms 2" × 5¾".

DARK TURQUOISE

Cut 4 squares 3" × 3"; cut in half diagonally.

DARK BLUE

Cut 4 squares 3" × 3"; cut in half diagonally.

LIGHT RUST

Cut 8 squares 5⅜" × 5⅜"; cut in half diagonally.

SMALL SIDE BLOCK

Finished size: 4½" × 4½"
Make 4 blocks.

OFF-WHITE

Cut 10 squares 2⅜" × 2⅜"; cut in half diagonally.

GREEN

Cut 6 squares 2⅜" × 2⅜"; cut in half diagonally.

DARK RUST/TURQUOISE

Cut 4 squares 2" × 2".

DARK TURQUOISE

Cut 8 trapezoids 2" × 3⅞".

DARK BLUE

Cut 4 squares 2" × 2".

CORNER TRIANGLE

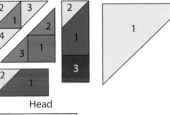

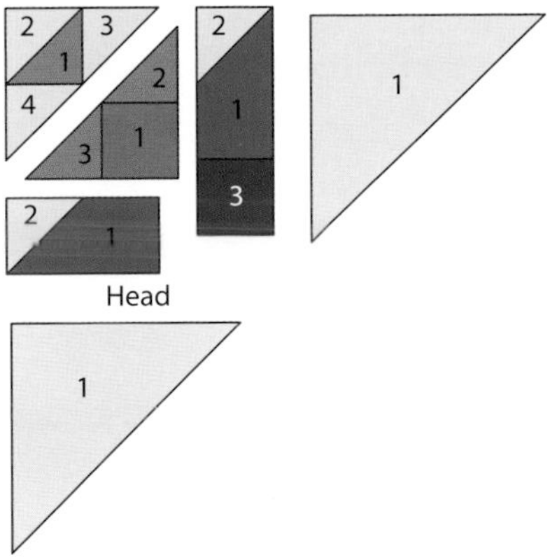

Head

Finished size: 6⅜" block, 12¾"
completed triangle
Make 4 blocks.

OFF-WHITE

1. Cut 10 squares 3" × 3"; cut in half diagonally.

2. Cut 4 squares 7¼" × 7¼"; cut in half diagonally.

GREEN

Cut 6 squares 3" × 3"; cut in half diagonally.

DARK RUST/TURQUOISE

Cut 4 squares 2⅝" × 2⅝".

DARK TURQUOISE

Cut 8 trapezoids 2⅝" × 5½".

DARK BLUE

Cut 4 squares 2⅝" × 2⅝".

Quilt Construction

Assembly diagram

Press carefully as each piece is sewn.

1. Sew the 4 center blocks together.

2. Sew 2 side rectangles to opposite sides of the center blocks.

3. Sew a small side block to each end of the remaining side rectangles. Sew these to the sides of the center blocks.

4. Cut 4 strips 3¾″ × 16⅝″ of off-white.

5. Cut 4 strips 3¾″ × 19⅞″ of off-white.

6. Trim an end of each strip at a 45° angle to make trapezoids.

7. Sew the 3¾″ × 16⅝″ strips to an outside edge of each corner triangle.

8. Sew the 3¾″ × 19⅞″ strips to the other outside edge of each corner triangle.

9. Sew the bordered corner triangles to the quilt.

Quilting

Decorative stitches are used to enhance the quilt motifs while serving as quilting stitches. Also, conventional quilting has been used.

midsummer's day dance

Quilt size: 68˝ × 68˝
Finished block sizes: 9˝ × 9˝, 12¾˝ × 12¾˝, 18˝ × 18˝

Materials

- Light green: ⅞ yard
- Rust: ½ yard
- Dark green: 1 yard (including borders)
- Light blue: ¾ yard
- Medium violet: ⅓ yard
- Light gold: ½ yard
- Medium light green: ¾ yard
- Yellow/violet floral: 1⅓ yards (including borders)
- Apricot/blue batik: 1¾ yards (including borders)
- Binding: ⅔ yard
- Backing: 4⅛ yards
- Batting: 72˝ × 72˝

CENTER BLOCK

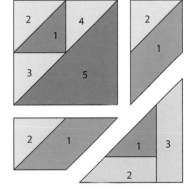

Finished size: 9˝ × 9˝
Make 4 blocks.

LIGHT GREEN

Cut 10 squares 3⅞˝ × 3⅞˝; cut in half diagonally.

This quilt, which uses Dragonfly Block 5, is a nine patch. It features a Dragonfly block turned on point, double wing blocks, and head blocks. A secondary star motif is possible from the triangle blocks surrounding the Dragonfly blocks. The light blue sections of the quilt are made from velveteen, which adds a visual dimension that would not be possible with plain cotton fabric.

Because both the parallelograms and trapezoids are mirror images in the block,

cut half of each shape angled right and half angled left. Make the blocks following the Dragonfly Block 5 piecing order on page 22.

RUST
Cut 2 squares 3⅞″ × 3⅞″; cut in half diagonally.

DARK GREEN
Cut 2 squares 6⅞″ × 6⅞″; cut in half diagonally.

LIGHT BLUE
Cut 8 parallelograms 2⅝″ × 7⅝″.

MEDIUM VIOLET
Cut 2 squares 3⅞″ × 3⅞″; cut in half diagonally.

LIGHT GOLD
1. Cut 4 trapezoids 2″ × 5⅜″.
2. Cut 4 trapezoids 2″ × 6⅞″.

SIDE BLOCK

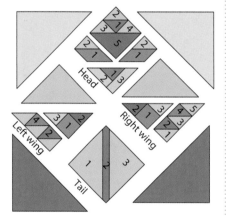

Finished size: 18″ × 18″
Small block size: 12¾″ × 12¾″
Make 4 blocks.

tip

The actual math for these blocks involves 1⁄16″ and 1⁄32″ measurements, which are really impractical for a quilter. The solution is to sew with a very scant ¼″ seam allowance: a couple of threads shy of ¼″.

RUST
1. Cut 6 squares 3″ × 3″; cut in half diagonally.
2. Cut 2 rectangles 1¼″ × 9¾″.

DARK GREEN
1. Cut 4 squares 3″ × 3″; cut in half diagonally.
2. Cut 2 squares 5⅛″ × 5⅛″; cut in half diagonally.

LIGHT BLUE
1. Cut 8 parallelograms 2″ × 5¾″.
2. Cut 8 squares 2⅝″ × 2⅝″.

MEDIUM VIOLET
Cut 6 squares 3″ × 3″; cut in half diagonally.

LIGHT GOLD
1. Cut 4 trapezoids 1½″ × 4⅛″.
2. Cut 4 trapezoids 1½″ × 5⅛″.
3. Cut 4 squares 3″ × 3″; cut in half diagonally.

MEDIUM-LIGHT GREEN
1. Cut 4 squares 6¾″ × 6¾″; cut in half diagonally.
2. Cut 4 squares 7¼″ × 7¼″; cut in half diagonally.
3. Cut 22 squares 3″ × 3″; cut in half diagonally.

APRICOT/BLUE BATIK
Cut 4 squares 9⅞″ × 9⅞″; cut in half diagonally.

YELLOW/VIOLET FLORAL
Cut 4 squares 9⅞″ × 9⅞″; cut in half diagonally.

CORNER BLOCK

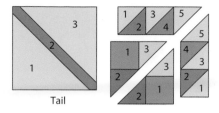

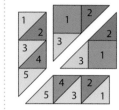

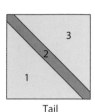

Finished size: 18″ × 18″
Make 4 blocks.

LIGHT GREEN
1. Cut 4 squares 9⅛″ × 9⅛″; cut in half diagonally.
2. Cut 24 squares 3⅞″ × 3⅞″; cut in half diagonally.

RUST
1. Cut 8 rectangles 1½″ × 13½″.
2. Cut 8 squares 3⅞″ × 3⅞″; cut in half diagonally.

DARK GREEN
Cut 8 squares 3⅞″ × 3⅞″; cut in half diagonally.

LIGHT BLUE
Cut 16 squares 3½″ × 3½″.

MEDIUM VIOLET
Cut 8 squares 3⅞″ × 3⅞″; cut in half diagonally.

LIGHT GOLD
Cut 8 squares 3⅞″ × 3⅞″; cut in half diagonally.

APRICOT/BLUE BATIK
Cut 4 squares 9⅛″ × 9⅛″; cut in half diagonally.

Quilt Construction

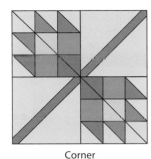
Corner

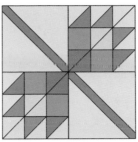
Side

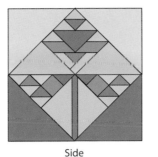
Corner

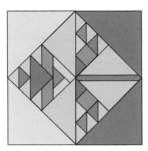
Side

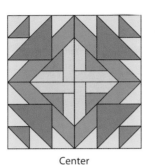
Center

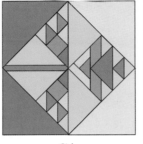
Side

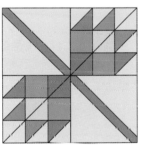
Corner

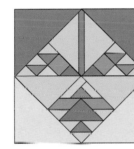
Side

Corner

Assembly diagram

Press carefully as each piece is sewn.

1. Sew the 4 center blocks together.

2. Arrange and sew the center, side, and corner blocks into 3 rows.

3. Sew the 3 rows together.

4. Make 2 border strips 3″ × 54½″ of yellow/violet floral. Sew to the sides of the quilt.

5. Make 2 border strips 3″ × 59½″ of yellow/violet floral. Sew to the top and bottom of the quilt.

6. Make 2 border strips 1½″ × 59½″ of dark green. Sew to the sides of the quilt.

7. Make 2 border strips 1½″ × 61½″ of dark green. Sew to the top and bottom of the quilt.

8. Make 2 border strips 4″ × 61½″ of apricot/blue batik. Sew to the sides of the quilt.

9. Make 2 border strips 4″ × 68½″ of apricot/blue batik. Sew to the top and bottom of the quilt.

Quilting

Decorative stitches enhance parts of the quilt block, while emphasizing the secondary motifs. They also serve as quilting stitches

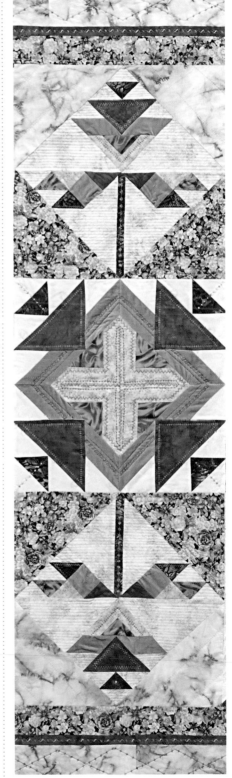

dragonfly in the sun

Quilt size: 76˝ × 76˝
Finished block size: 12˝ × 12˝

Materials

- Medium pink batik: 1¼ yards
- Dark red: 1¼ yards
- Light pink batik: 1¼ yards
- Medium blue batik: 1 yard
- Dark apricot/rose batik: ⅝ yard
- Light green floral: 1 yard
- White: 2⅔ yards
- Medium rust: ¾ yard
- Dark pink floral: ¾ yard
- Light apricot batik: ½ yard
- Light pink/green floral: ⅔ yard
- Dark rust sashing: ⅞ yard
- Binding: ¾ yard
- Backing: 4½ yards
- Batting: 80˝ × 80˝

This quilt uses Dragonfly Block 6. The floral fabrics and white background create a large center motif, which almost obscures the individual Dragonfly motifs. Sashing strips create a border that frames the larger central design. Decorative stitches create an almost Victorian feel, and are an important part of this quilt.

Because the parallelograms are mirror images in the block, cut half of the pieces angled right and half angled left. Make the blocks following the Dragonfly Block 6 piecing order on page 22.

Decorative stitches

CENTER BLOCK

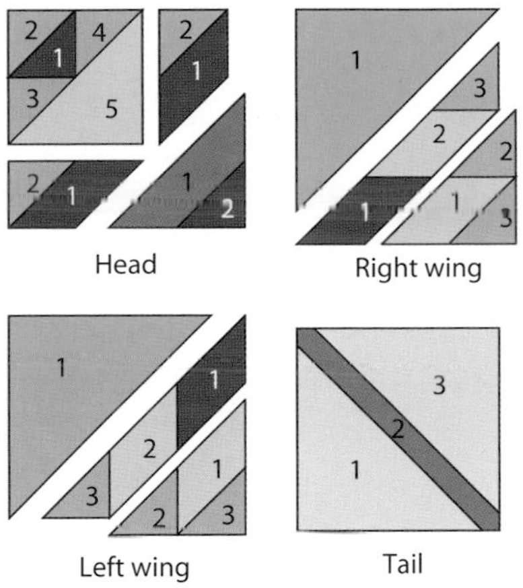

Head

Right wing

Left wing

Tail

Finished size: 12˝ × 12˝
Make 4 blocks.

MEDIUM PINK BATIK

Cut 22 squares 2⅞˝ × 2⅞˝; cut in half diagonally.

DARK RED

1. Cut 4 squares 2⅞˝ × 2⅞˝; cut in half diagonally

2. Cut 16 parallelograms 1⅞˝ × 5½˝.

LIGHT PINK BATIK

1. Cut 16 parallelograms 1⅞˝ × 5½˝.

2. Cut 2 squares 4⅞˝ × 4⅞˝; cut in half diagonally.

MEDIUM BLUE BATIK

1. Cut 4 rectangles 1¼˝ × 9¼˝

2. Cut 4 quadrilaterals 1⅞˝ × 6⅞˝.

DARK APRICOT/ROSE BATIK

Cut 4 squares 6⅞˝ × 6⅞˝; cut in half diagonally.

LIGHT GREEN FLORAL

Cut 4 squares 6⅜˝ × 6⅜˝; cut in half diagonally.

SIDE BLOCK A & B

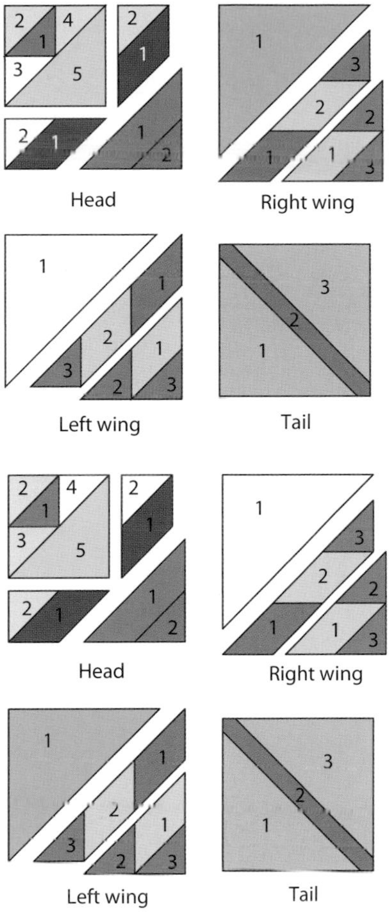

Head

Right wing

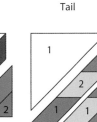

Left wing

Tail

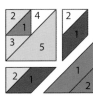

Head

Right wing

Left wing

Tail

Finished size: 12˝ × 12˝
Make 4 of each block.

DARK RED

Cut 16 parallelograms 1⅞˝ × 5½˝.

LIGHT PINK BATIK

1. Cut 4 squares 4⅞˝ × 4⅞˝; cut in half diagonally.

2. Cut 32 parallelograms 1⅞˝ × 5½˝.

MEDIUM BLUE BATIK

1. Cut 16 parallelograms 1⅞˝ × 5½˝.

2. Cut 4 squares 2⅞˝ × 2⅞˝; cut in half diagonally.

3. Cut 8 rectangles 1¼˝ × 9¼˝.

DARK APRICOT/ROSE BATIK

Cut 4 squares 6⅞˝ × 6⅞˝; cut in half diagonally.

LIGHT GREEN FLORAL

Cut 12 squares 2⅞˝ × 2⅞˝; cut in half diagonally.

WHITE

1. Cut 8 squares 2⅞˝ × 2⅞˝; cut in half diagonally.

2. Cut 4 squares 6⅞˝ × 6⅞˝; cut in half diagonally.

MEDIUM RUST

1. Cut 28 squares 2⅞˝ × 2⅞˝; cut in half diagonally.

2. Cut 8 quadrilaterals 1⅞˝ × 6⅞˝.

DARK PINK FLORAL

Cut 8 squares 6⅜˝ × 6⅜˝; cut in half diagonally.

CORNER BLOCK

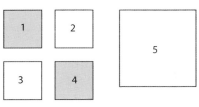
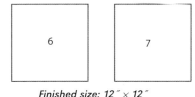

Finished size: 12˝ × 12˝
Make 4 blocks.

LIGHT PINK BATIK

Cut 8 squares 3½˝ × 3½˝.

WHITE

1. Cut 12 squares 6½˝ × 6½˝.

2. Cut 8 squares 3½˝ × 3½˝.

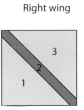

BORDER BLOCK A

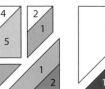

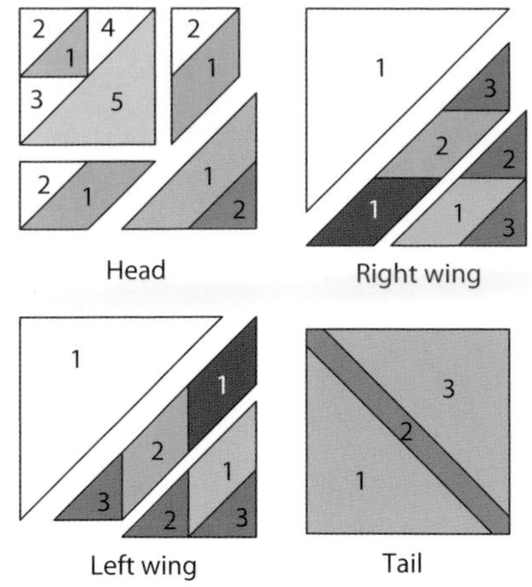

Head

Right wing

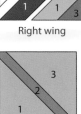

Left wing

Tail

Finished size: 12˝ × 12˝
Make 8 blocks.

MEDIUM PINK BATIK

Cut 32 parallelograms 1⅞˝ × 5½˝.

DARK RED

Cut 16 parallelograms 1⅞˝ × 5½˝.

LIGHT PINK BATIK

Cut 4 squares 4⅞˝ × 4⅞˝; cut in half diagonally.

MEDIUM BLUE BATIK

1. Cut 8 rectangles 1¼˝ × 9¼˝.

2. Cut 4 squares 2⅞˝ × 2⅞˝; cut in half diagonally.

LIGHT GREEN FLORAL

Cut 8 quadrilaterals 1⅞˝ × 6⅞˝.

WHITE

1. Cut 20 squares 2⅞˝ × 2⅞˝; cut in half diagonally.

2. Cut 8 squares 6⅞˝ × 6⅞˝; cut in half diagonally.

MEDIUM RUST

Cut 24 squares 2⅞˝ × 2⅞˝; cut in half diagonally.

DARK PINK FLORAL

1. Cut 4 squares 2⅞˝ × 2⅞˝; cut in half diagonally.

2. Cut 8 squares 6⅜˝ × 6⅜˝; cut in half diagonally.

LIGHT APRICOT BATIK

Cut 16 parallelograms 1⅞˝ × 5½˝.

BORDER BLOCK B

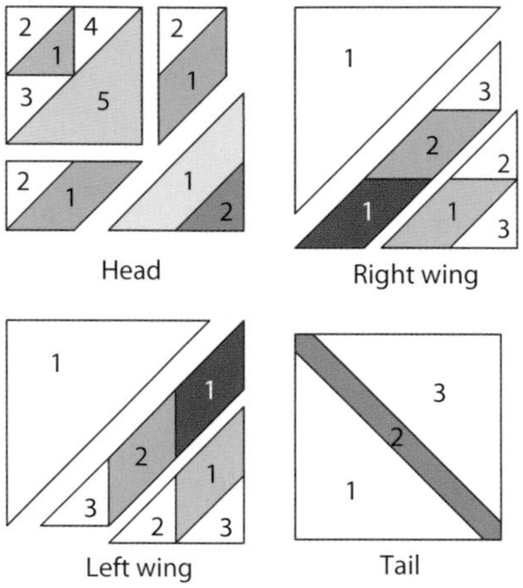

Head

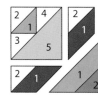

Right wing

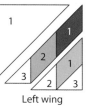

Left wing

Tail

Finished size: 12˝ × 12˝
Make 8 blocks.

MEDIUM PINK BATIK

Cut 32 parallelograms 1⅞˝ × 5½˝.

DARK RED

Cut 16 parallelograms 1⅞˝ × 5½˝.

LIGHT PINK BATIK

Cut 4 squares 4⅞˝ × 4⅞˝; cut in half diagonally.

MEDIUM BLUE BATIK

1. Cut 8 rectangles 1¼˝ × 9¼˝.

2. Cut 4 squares 2⅞˝ × 2⅞˝; cut in half diagonally.

LIGHT GREEN FLORAL

Cut 8 quadrilaterals 1⅞˝ × 6⅞˝.

WHITE

1. Cut 44 squares 2⅞˝ × 2⅞˝; cut in half diagonally.

2. Cut 8 squares 6⅞˝ × 6⅞˝; cut in half diagonally.

3. Cut 8 squares 6⅜˝ × 6⅜˝; cut in half diagonally.

DARK PINK FLORAL

Cut 4 squares 2⅞˝ × 2⅞˝; cut in half diagonally.

LIGHT APRICOT BATIK

Cut 16 parallelograms 1⅞˝ × 5½˝.

BORDER CORNER

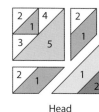

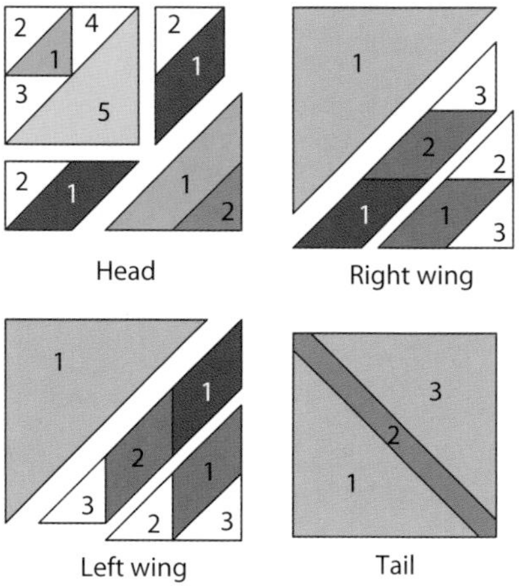

Head

Right wing

Left wing

Tail

Finished size: 12˝ × 12˝
Make 4 blocks.

MEDIUM PINK BATIK

1. Cut 2 squares 2⅞˝ × 2⅞˝; cut in half diagonally.

2. Cut 4 quadrilaterals 1⅞˝ × 6⅞˝.

DARK RED

Cut 16 parallelograms 1⅞˝ × 5½˝.

LIGHT PINK BATIK

Cut 2 squares 4⅞˝ × 4⅞˝; cut in half diagonally.

MEDIUM BLUE BATIK

1. Cut 4 rectangles 1¼˝ × 9¼˝.

2. Cut 2 squares 2⅞˝ × 2⅞˝; cut in half diagonally.

WHITE

Cut 22 squares 2⅞″ × 2⅞″; cut in half diagonally.

MEDIUM RUST

Cut 16 parallelograms 1⅞″ × 5½″.

LIGHT GREEN/PINK FLORAL

1. Cut 4 squares 6⅞″ × 6⅞″; cut in half diagonally.

2. Cut 4 squares 6⅜″ × 6⅜″; cut in half diagonally.

6. Cut 4 strips 2½″ × 12½″ of dark rust. Arrange and sew the remaining border blocks and strips to make the side borders. Sew to the sides of the quilt.

Quilt Construction

Assembly diagram

1. Arrange and sew the center, side, and corner blocks into 4 rows.

2. Sew the rows together to make the center section of the quilt.

3. Make 2 border strips 2½″ × 48½″ of dark rust. Sew to the top and bottom of the center section.

4. Arrange and sew border blocks A and B to make the top and bottom borders. Sew to the quilt center.

5. Make 2 border strips 2½″ × 76½″ of dark rust. Sew to the sides of the center section.

Quilting

This quilt features mainly decorative stitches. These stitches are an integral part of the quilt design, producing an almost Victorian flavor. The sections of white background are heavily quilted, which brings out the leaf design.

sundial

Quilt size: 45˝ × 45˝
Finished block size: 15˝ × 15˝

This quilt uses Dragonfly Block 5 and is constructed as a nine patch. There are 4 full Dragonfly blocks. The side blocks are composed of only the head section of the Dragonfly block. The center block is made from 4 mirrored double wing blocks, which have been modified: instead of 8 triangles, 16 small squares lie at the very center of the block.

Because both the parallelograms and trapezoids are mirror images in the block, cut half the pieces for each shape angled right and half angled left. Make the blocks following the Dragonfly Block 5 piecing order on page 22.

Materials

■ Violet/green floral: 1¼ yards

■ Red/violet: ⅜ yard

■ Dark blue: ⅜ yard

■ Green: ½ yard

■ Violet/blue/pink: ¼ yard

■ Violet: ⅛ yard

■ Turquoise: ⅜ yard

■ Light blue: 1½ yards

■ Binding: ⅝ yard

■ Backing: 2¾ yards

■ Batting: 49˝ × 49˝

CENTER BLOCK

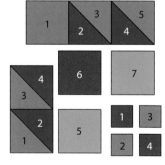

Finished size: 7½˝ × 7½˝
Make 4 blocks.

VIOLET/GREEN FLORAL

1. Cut 4 squares 3˝ × 3˝.

2. Cut 8 squares 3⅜˝ × 3⅜˝; cut in half diagonally.

RED/VIOLET

1. Cut 4 squares 3″ × 3″.
2. Cut 4 squares 3⅜″ × 3⅜″; cut in half diagonally.
3. Cut 4 squares 1¾″ × 1¾″.

DARK BLUE

Cut 4 squares 3⅜″ × 3⅜″; cut in half diagonally.

GREEN

Cut 8 squares 3″ × 3″.

VIOLET/BLUE/PINK

Cut 8 squares 1¾″ × 1¾″.

VIOLET

Cut 4 squares 1¾″ × 1¾″.

SIDE BLOCK A

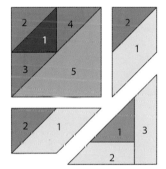

Finished size: 7½″ × 7½″
Make 8 blocks.

VIOLET/GREEN FLORAL

Cut 20 squares 3⅜″ × 3⅜″; cut in half diagonally.

DARK BLUE

Cut 4 squares 3⅜″ × 3⅜″; cut in half diagonally.

GREEN

Cut 4 squares 5⅞″ × 5⅞″; cut in half diagonally.

TURQUOISE

Cut 4 squares 3⅜″ × 3⅜″; cut in half diagonally.

LIGHT BLUE

1. Cut 16 parallelograms 2¼″ × 6½″.
2. Cut 8 trapezoids 1¾″ × 4⅝″.
3. Cut 8 trapezoids 1¾″ × 5⅞″.

SIDE BLOCK B

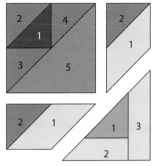

Finished size: 7½″ × 7½″
Make 8 blocks.

VIOLET/GREEN FLORAL

Cut 20 squares 3⅜″ × 3⅜″; cut in half diagonally.

RED/VIOLET

Cut 4 squares 3⅜″ × 3⅜″; cut in half diagonally.

GREEN

Cut 4 squares 3⅜″ × 3⅜″; cut in half diagonally.

TURQUOISE

Cut 4 squares 5⅞″ × 5⅞″; cut in half diagonally.

LIGHT BLUE

1. Cut 16 parallelograms 2¼″ × 6½″.
2. Cut 8 trapezoids 1¾″ × 5⅞″.
3. Cut 8 trapezoids 1¾″ × 4⅝″.

CORNER BLOCK

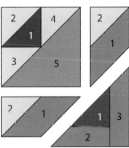

Head
Right wing
Left wing
Tail

Finished size: 15″ × 15″
Make 4 blocks.

VIOLET/GREEN FLORAL

1. Cut 8 parallelograms 2¼″ × 6½″.
2. Cut 8 trapezoids 1¾″ × 5⅞″.
3. Cut 8 trapezoids 1¾″ × 4⅝″.

RED/VIOLET

Cut 2 squares 3⅜″ × 3⅜″; cut in half diagonally.

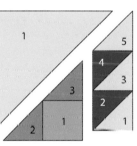

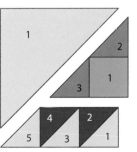

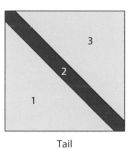

DARK BLUE

1. Cut 10 squares 3⅜″ × 3⅜″; cut in half diagonally.

2. Cut 4 rectangles 1⅜″ × 11⅜″.

VIOLET/BLUE/PINK

Cut 8 squares 3⅜″ × 3⅜″; cut in half diagonally.

TURQUOISE

Cut 2 squares 5⅞″ × 5⅞″; cut in half diagonally.

LIGHT BLUE

1. Cut 22 squares 3⅜″ × 3⅜″; cut in half diagonally.

2. Cut 4 squares 8⅜″ × 8⅜″; cut in half diagonally.

3. Cut 4 squares 7¾″ × 7¾″; cut in half diagonally.

GREEN

Cut 8 squares 3″ × 3″.

Press carefully as each piece is sewn.

1. Sew the 4 center blocks together.

2. Arrange and sew 2 each of side blocks A and B to make the side blocks.

3. Arrange and sew the center, side, and corner blocks together in 3 rows.

5. Sew the rows together.

Quilt Construction

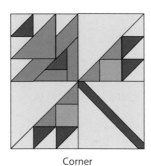
Corner

Side

Corner

Side

Center

Side

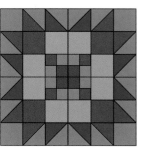
Corner

Side

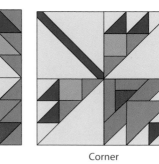
Corner

Assembly diagram

Quilting

Contour stitching has been chosen to emphasize specific large motifs. Stitch-in-the-ditch quilting is used in the remainder of the quilt.

loop-de-loop

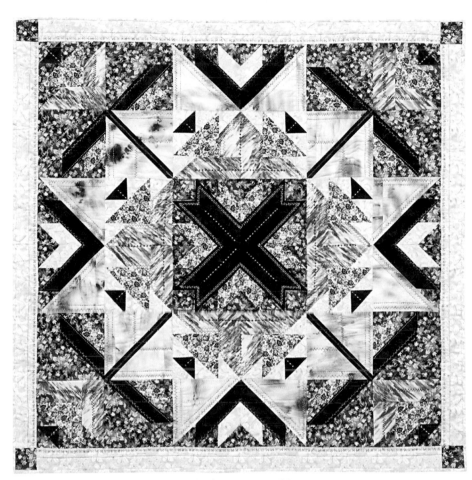

Quilt size: 50˝ × 50˝
Finished block sizes: 7½˝ × 7½˝, 15˝ × 15˝

This quilt uses Dragonfly Block 3. The quilt is blue, but it actually has touches of other colors in the fabric and in the quilting thread. This gives it zest. The dark blue central × of the double wing block is echoed in the other wing blocks in the quilt. There is a secondary image that is reminiscent of an Eight-Pointed Star. The quilt has a border band with squares at the corners.

Because both the parallelograms and trapezoids are mirror images in the block,

cut half the pieces for each shape angled right and half angled left. Make the blocks following the Dragonfly Block 3 piecing order on page 21.

Materials

- Dark blue floral: 1 yard (including border squares)
- Medium blue floral: ¾ yard
- Dark blue: ⅞ yard
- Light blue floral: 1 yard (including borders)
- Medium blue: ⅔ yard
- Light blue: ⅔ yard
- Binding: ⅝ yard
- Backing: 3⅛ yards
- Batting: 54˝ × 54˝

CENTER BLOCK

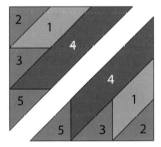

Finished size: 7½˝ × 7½˝
Make 4 blocks.

DARK BLUE FLORAL

Cut 12 squares 3⅜˝ × 3⅜˝; cut in half diagonally.

MEDIUM BLUE FLORAL

Cut 8 parallelograms 2¼˝ × 6½˝.

DARK BLUE

Cut 8 parallelograms 2¼˝ × 10⅛˝.

SIDE BLOCK

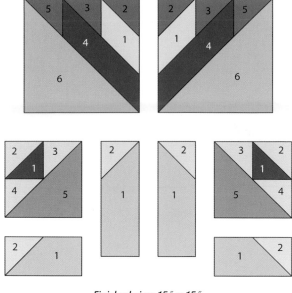

Finished size: 15″ × 15″
Make 4 blocks.

DARK BLUE FLORAL

Cut 12 squares 3⅜″ × 3⅜″; cut in half diagonally.

MEDIUM BLUE FLORAL

Cut 4 squares 5⅞″ × 5⅞″; cut in half diagonally.

DARK BLUE

1. Cut 4 squares 3⅜″ × 3⅜″; cut in half diagonally.
2. Cut 8 parallelograms 2¼″ × 10⅛″.

LIGHT BLUE FLORAL

1. Cut 20 squares 3⅜″ × 3⅜″; cut in half diagonally.
2. Cut 8 parallelograms 2¼″ × 6½″.

MEDIUM BLUE

1. Cut 8 trapezoids 3″ × 5⅞″.
2. Cut 8 trapezoids 3″ × 8⅜″.

LIGHT BLUE

Cut 4 squares 8⅜″ × 8⅜″; cut in half diagonally.

CORNER BLOCK

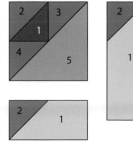

Head
Right wing
Left wing
Tail

Finished size: 15″ × 15″
Make 4 blocks.

DARK BLUE FLORAL

1. Cut 22 squares 3⅜″ × 3⅜″; cut in half diagonally.
2. Cut 4 squares 8⅜″ × 8⅜″; cut in half diagonally.

MEDIUM BLUE FLORAL

1. Cut 2 squares 5⅞″ × 5⅞″; cut in half diagonally.
2. Cut 8 parallelograms 2¼″ × 6½″.

DARK BLUE

1. Cut 2 squares 3⅜″ × 3⅜″; cut in half diagonally.
2. Cut 8 parallelograms 2¼″ × 10⅛″.
3. Cut 4 rectangles 1⅜″ × 11⅜″.

MEDIUM BLUE

1. Cut 4 trapezoids 3″ × 5⅞″.
2. Cut 4 trapezoids 3″ × 8⅜″.

LIGHT BLUE

Cut 4 squares 7⅝″ × 7⅝″; cut in half diagonally.

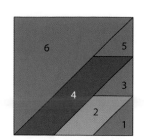

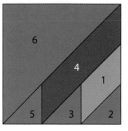

Quilt Construction

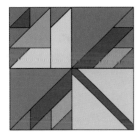
Corner

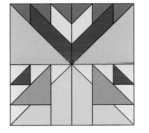
Corner

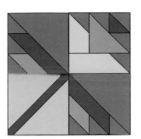
Side

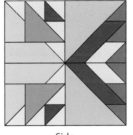
Corner

Side

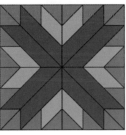
Center

Side

Side

Corner

Side

Corner

Assembly diagram

Press carefully as each piece is sewn.

1. Sew the 4 center blocks together.

2. Arrange and sew the center, side, and corner blocks into 3 rows.

3. Sew the rows together.

4. Make 2 border strips 3″ × 45½″ of light blue floral. Sew to the sides of the quilt.

5. Make 2 border strips 3″ × 45½″ of light blue floral.

6. Cut 4 squares 3″ × 3″ of dark blue floral.

7. Sew the 3″ squares to the ends of the remaining 3″ × 45½″ border strips. Sew to the top and bottom of the quilt.

Quilting

A mix of decorative stitches and traditional quilting stitches complement this quilt.

gallery

Dragonflower *by Anne Kinnel*

Centered motifs and bright colors make this quilt dance and sing. This quilt, based on All Aflutter *(page 63), uses Block 5.—Sue Beevers*

A tropical floral print with coordinating fabrics creates a nine-block quilt that retains the Dragonfly image but is more about color choices and placement. However, much of the quilting does suggest insect flight. The blocks are 18″ square, so the quilt is close to 60″ with the small border.

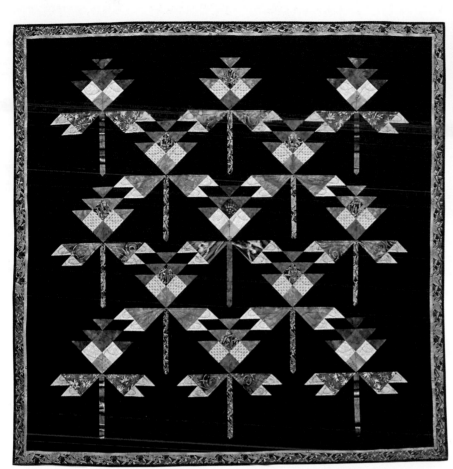

Midnight Metamorphosis
by Margaret Willemsen,
machine quilted by Karol Kleppe

Block 1 on a black background and turned on point creates a stunning quilt.—Sue Beevers

Margaret asked Karol to imagine the black background as water. After years in a watery home, the dragonfly nymph heads for shore and, often under the cover of night, metamorphoses into a beautiful dragonfly.

Journey Through the Sky Hole
by Margaret Willemsen,
machine quilted by Karol Kleppe

With five Block 1's turned on point, the subtle colors of the four corner blocks create the fascinating illusion of dragonflies swirling.—Sue Beevers

My inspiration was a Zuni legend about the origins of the Dragonfly. The goal was to evoke memory, landscape, and tradition.

Dragonfly Quilt *by Gail Strout*

What a difference colors and setting make! This wonderful quilt uses Block 6 in the Sundial *setting (page 84). —Sue Beevers*

I wanted high contrast while choosing fabrics for the initial pattern of Sue Beevers' design. When I decided to enlarge the quilt to bed size, I continued the Dragonfly motif but altered the orientation of the blocks to make a defined edge in the same color range. I also wanted the basic block design more apparent.

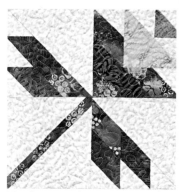

Meadowsweet *by Kathryn Stenstrom*

High contrast and beautiful fabrics create this striking quilt, which uses Block 6 and the same layout as Dragonfly Moon *(page 71).—Sue Beevers*

I made a very straightforward quilt to emphasize the beauty of the setting, using a large-scale print to dramatize the geometry created by the path of the tail blocks. Other fabrics were chosen to suggest a summer meadow.

Dragonfly Square Dance: Promenade
Round and Do-Si-Do to the Corners
by Paula Schultz,
machine quilted by Lorraine Kabot

Blank spaces are used as a blackboard for
drawing dragonflies and their flight paths. This
quilt uses Block 6 in the same setting as Oasis
(page 60).—Sue Beevers

The overall style of the block inspired the name.
I wanted to use two Australian fabrics, and the
yellow print and red border were my starting
point. The green was added to spark the design
up. I usually do not do patterns that have so much
blank space, so that was very challenging. It was
custom machine quilted by Lorraine Kabot.

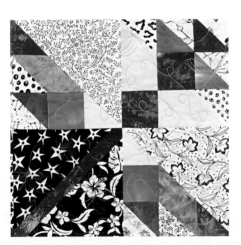

Dragonflies Dancing *by Sue Ellen Romanowski*

Simple primary colors along with black-
and-white fabrics create this fun-loving
quilt that uses Block 2 and is based on
the example on page 31.—Sue Beevers

ABOUT THE AUTHOR

Sue Beevers knows her life is a creative journey.

Playing with fiber all of her life, Sue started out as a weaver, dyer, and spinner, and has written articles, taught workshops, and had her work featured in five books on these topics. Her creativity extends into art and music. As the violoncello instructor at Hamilton College in upstate New York, she also sews, knits, crochets, and tats—but since discovering painting and quilting, she has never looked back.

Sue says her life revolves around being outdoors. Her major interest is the natural cycles in the world—the seasonal changes and the cycles of growing things.

She loves teaching classes. Her biggest kick in life is to watch people take something they already know and look at it differently.

Sue has been married to David for more than 30 years. She has two grown children and two grandchildren. She teaches quilting and fabric painting and designs fabrics for RJR Fabrics. This is her second book with C&T Publishing. Visit her at *www.suebeevers.com*.

RESOURCES

Janome America, Inc.
10 Industrial Ave
Mahwah, NJ 07430
(800) 631-0183
www.janome.com

Mountain Mist
P.O. Box 44427
Tacoma, WA 98448
(800) 232-7332
www.mountainmistlp.com

RJR Fabrics
2203 Dominguez St—Building K-3
Torrance, CA 90501
(800) 422-5426
www.rjrfabrics.com

Sulky of America
980 Cobb Place Blvd—Ste 130
Kennesaw, GA 30144
(800) 874-4115
www.sulky.com

For a list of other fine books from
C&T Publishing, ask for a free catalog:

C&T Publishing, Inc.
P.O. Box 1456
Lafayette, CA 94549
(800) 284-1114
Email: ctinfo@ctpub.com
Website: www.ctpub.com

C&T Publishing's professional
photography services are now
available to the public. Visit us at
www.ctmediaservices.com.

For quilting supplies:
Cotton Patch
1025 Brown Ave.
Lafayette, CA 94549
Store: (925) 284-1177
Mail order: (925) 283-7883
Email: CottonPa@aol.com
Website: www.quiltusa.com

Great Titles

from C&T PUBLISHING

Available at your local retailer or

www.ctpub.com or 800.284.1114